"Several governments in the West have grown committed to exporting religious freedom worldwide and have looked at the United States for inspiration. While explaining why the American model has been on the rise since the 1998 International Religious Freedom Act, Pasquale Annicchino suggests that international politics subservient to national interests are threatening the global religious conversation."

Professor Marco Ventura, University of Siena, Italy

"*Law and International Religious Freedom* is a sophisticated study in how (mostly conservative) conceptions of religious liberty have been exported to Europe from the United States and are influencing the development of European church/state law. Dr Annicchino possesses a deep knowledge of multiple legal systems which he deploys in a nuanced analysis of the dissemination of a particular conception of religious liberty in Europe by theologically conservative religions in the US. Appearing for the first time in English, in the midst of the US's apparent cession of global leadership following the election of President Trump, Annicchino's examination of this phenomenon could not be more timely. Everyone concerned with the current state of religious freedom at home and abroad will want to read this book."

Frederick M. Gedicks, Brigham Young University, USA

Law and International Religious Freedom: The Rise and Decline of the American Model was originally published in Italian in 2015 by Società editrice il Mulino with the title *Esportare la libertà religiosa. Il Modello Americano nell'Arena Globale* © 2015 by Società editrice il Mulino, Bologna.

Law and International Religious Freedom

This book analyzes the promotion and protection of freedom of religion in the international arena with a particular focus on the role and influence of the US International Religious Freedom Act, 1998. It also investigates the impact of the IRFA on the legislation and policies of third countries and the EU. The book develops the story of the protection of religious freedom through foreign policy by showing how religious laws affect and shape a more communitarian dimension of the notion of freedom of religion which stands in contrast with a traditionally Western individualistic understanding of the right. It is argued that it is still possible to defend the unstable category of freedom of religion or belief especially when major violations are at stake. The book presents a balanced contribution to the academic debate on the promotion and protection of religious freedom. The comparative approach and interdisciplinary methodology make it a valuable resource for academics, students and policy-makers in Law, International Relations and Strategic Studies.

Dr Pasquale Annicchino is a Visiting Fellow in the Robert Schuman Centre for Advanced Studies, European University Institute, Italy and a Senior Research Associate at the Cambridge Institute on Religion and International Studies, Cambridge, United Kingdom. His research interests are in the areas of Law and Religion, Comparative Human Rights, National Security Law, Legal Theory, and European Union Law and EU External Relations. He has published widely on these and related areas.

ICLARS Series on Law and Religion

Series Editors:

Silvio Ferrari, University of Milan, Italy, Russell Sandberg, Cardiff University, UK, Pieter Coertzen, University of Stellenbosch, South Africa, W. Cole Durham, Jr., Brigham Young University, USA, and Tahir Mahmood, Amity International University, India

The *ICLARS Series on Law and Religion* is a new series designed to provide a forum for the rapidly expanding field of research in law and religion. The series is published in association with the International Consortium for Law and Religion Studies, an international network of scholars and experts of law and religion founded in 2007 with the aim of providing a place where information, data and opinions can easily be exchanged among members and made available to the broader scientific community. The series aims to become a primary source for students and scholars while presenting authors with a valuable means to reach a wide and growing readership.

Other titles in this series

Blasphemy, Islam and the State
Stewart Fenwick, University of Melbourne, Australia

Religions and Constitutional Transitions in the Muslim Mediterranean
Edited by Alessandro Ferrari, University of Insubria, Italy and James Toronto, Brigham Young University, USA

Religion, Pluralism, and Reconciling Difference
W. Cole Durham, Jr. and Donlu Thayer, both at Brigham Young University, USA

Religion and Equality
Edited by W. Cole Durham, Jr. and Donlu Thayer, both at Brigham Young University, USA

Church and State in Scotland
Francis Lyall, University of Aberdeen, UK

Religion as Empowerment
Edited by Kyriaki Topidi and Lauren Fielder, both at University of Lucerne, Switzerland

www.routledge.com/ICLARS-Series-on-Law-and-Religion/book-series/ICLARS

Law and International Religious Freedom

The Rise and Decline of the American Model

Pasquale Annicchino

Routledge
Taylor & Francis Group
LONDON AND NEW YORK

First published 2018 by Routledge

2 Park Square, Milton Park, Abingdon, Oxfordshire OX14 4RN
52 Vanderbilt Avenue, New York, NY 10017

Routledge is an imprint of the Taylor & Francis Group, an informa business

First issued in paperback 2019

Translated by Chiara Di Benedetto Brown

Law and International Religious Freedom: The Rise and Decline of the American Model was originally published in Italian in 2015 by Società editrice il Mulino with the title *Esportare la libertà religiosa. Il Modello Americano nell'Arena Globale* © 2015 by Società editrice il Mulino, Bologna.

British Library Cataloguing-in-Publication Data
A catalogue record for this book is available from the British Library

Library of Congress Cataloging-in-Publication Data
Names: Annicchino, Pasquale, author. | Brown, Chiara Di Benedetto. translator.
Title: Law and international religious freedom : the rise and decline of the
American model / Pasquale Annicchino ; translated by Chiara Di Benedetto Brown.
Other titles: Esportare la libertáa religiosa. English
Description: Abingdon, Oxon ; New York, NY : Routledge, 2018. |
Includes bibliographical references and index.
Identifiers: LCCN 2017034752 | ISBN 9781138282445 (hardback)
Subjects: LCSH: United States. International Religious Freedom Act of 1998. |
United States–Foreign relations–Law and legislation. | Freedom of religion
(International law) | Freedom of religion–European Union countries. |
Law–American influences.
Classification: LCC KF4650.A328 1998 A5613 2018 | DDC 341.4/832–dc23
LC record available at https://lccn.loc.gov/2017034752

ISBN: 978-1-138-28244-5 (hbk)
ISBN: 978-0-367-88609-7 (pbk)

Typeset in Galliard
by Out of House Publishing

Contents

Preface to the English edition

This book is the translation from the Italian of a work published in 2015 by Il Mulino. I decided to maintain the original structure and content of the book as it appeared in the Italian version. Some references to the Italian literature have been deleted to facilitate reading by a non-Italian audience; quotations from Italian have been translated into English in order to facilitate non-native speakers. My interest in this particular field of law started in 2012, when I presented a paper at Harvard Law School at a conference organized by Prof. Marie Anne Glendon and Prof. Rafael Alvira. At that time, the European Union was just beginning to develop an interest in the protection and promotion of freedom of religion in its external action. Talking to people who were working on this issue in Brussels, I could see that the United States was a model for many of them. It would have been impossible to duplicate the American model within the European Union, but some ideas originally developed in the United States began to circulate in Europe as well, and in June 2013 the European Council approved the EU Guidelines for the Promotion and Protection of Freedom of Religion or Belief in the external action of the European Union. Some states began to adopt their own policies of promotion and protection of religious freedom, at times creating conflicts and adding incoherence to the international system. In addition to the role of states, religious groups also began to push for a new understanding of religious freedom, both internally and in the international arena. This gave rise to a competition between different understandings of the nature and the scope of this right, a challenge we still face today. I have also added a postscript to the pages translated from the Italian edition. There I mention some new developments and assess the extent to which the model of protection and promotion of international religious freedom developed in the United States can still contribute to global efforts in this domain. I do not join the ranks of skeptics who claim that we could do without the very notion of a right to religious freedom. At the same time, I do think that – especially if Western countries continue to apply double standards, and menu à la carte – it will be very difficult to defend the relevance – and in fact, the very essence – of the right to religious freedom. We may very much be facing a decline of Western interest in religious freedom. This is especially problematic at a time when we are witnessing an increase in violations by national and supranational actors of the right to religious freedom and an increase in persecutions of religious minorities. This book therefore, without claiming to have found a definitive answer, aims to look at the debates on international religious freedom, above all from the legal perspective and with a constructive approach, without denying the problems at stake. It is an approach that I find very congenial to the path I have followed so far, formed through interactions with and the mentoring of different academics. I therefore would like to take this opportunity to thank some of them. It will be impossible to acknowledge all the direct and indirect contributions of all the people with whom I have exchanged opinions on this topic. First of all, I would like to thank Olivier Roy – I will never forget the day he hired me at the European University Institute, and how open and welcoming he has been toward me. He has contributed greatly, not only materially but especially intellectually, to making this book possible. In fact, the Italian edition of this book was published as part of his RELIGIOWEST research project. I should also acknowledge the constant support and mentoring of my Ph.D. supervisor, Marco Ventura, who has included me in several research projects and is always available when the questions become more difficult. Several colleagues at the European University Institute have also helped shape my ideas on some of the issues analyzed in this book: Maria Birnbaum, Nadia Marzouki, Luigi Narbone, and Kristina Stoeckl. I was very lucky to be able to share an office with Kristina, and I hope that our exchanges of ideas contributed to the shaping of her new project on Russia and the United States, to which I have been very glad to contribute. I have had the opportunity to test some of the ideas discussed in this book at several national and international workshops and conferences. Among the scholars based in Italy I would like to thank Gianfranco Macrì for his constant spirit of initiative and for involving me in several research projects, Susanna Mancini for her constant advice, Giuseppe Martinico, who is almost like an older brother to me, and Nicola Colaianni, Pierluigi Consorti Alessandro Ferrari, Nicola Fiorita, Roberto Mazzola, Vincenzo Pacillo, and Andrea Pin for participating and contributing in various ways at events where the ideas forming the basis of this book were discussed. Gabriele Fattori also deserves special mention, not only for his contributions to this book, but also for his constant stream of wise suggestions. Carlo Cantore spent numerous evenings and afternoons watching me work on the draft of this book, and has been a real friend to me over the years at the EUI.

Ideas (like people) do travel, and therefore I should also acknowledge the contributions and kindnesses of scholars based at other European universities: Lorenzo Zucca, for hosting me at his place several times and for the time spent in London during my fellowship at King's College, Peter Petkoff, always energetic and sharp in his critiques, Javier Martinez Tòrron for the kind invitation in Madrid, and Blandine Chelini-Pont, Marie-Claire Foblets, and Mark Hill for their invariable willingness to discuss any doubt or question.

This book could not have been written without the fundamental contributions gleaned from my many trips to the United States, and the wise advice of many scholars located there. I would like to thank my friends at Brigham Young University Law School: Fred Gedicks, whom I have known for many years, and who a few years ago was also a member of my Ph.D. defense panel. My months spent at BYU doing research and teaching as an adjunct professor have been of great help to the writing process. And of course it would be impossible not to mention Cole Durham and Brett Scharffs. Cole will always be a constant source of inspiration for his commitment to research and ability to interact with people of different cultures and backgrounds. Brett, who will now be serving as the new director of the BYU Center for the Study of Law and Religion, is probably the only person who could have taken over that enormous task from Cole. I am sure the Centre will continue to be a leading voice in the global debate on law and religion. Mark Movsesian and Marc Degirolami from St. John's Law School have been real friends to me as well, and I am sure we will have many other opportunities to co-organize events like the one we did in Trento. During my teaching period in New York I really felt at home, and this was mainly thanks to them. Zachary

Calo has also been of great help – I will never forget the days spent in Doha teaching Qatari students. Clifford Bob has been a real discovery for me – reading some of his work and talking to him made me realize that interdisciplinary research is truly possible. Last, but not least, Michael Rosenfeld – his door at Cardozo Law School has always been open. I hope to be able to work with him again in the future. I want to thank Silvio Ferrari and the editors of this series for accepting this book for publication. Prof. Ferrari is a role model for all young scholars who deal with this subject. His candid assessment of any draft we sent to him, his constant availability, and his willingness to involve young scholars in research are a constant reminder of what it should mean to be an academic. The global community of law and religion scholars owes much to him.

A special and well-deserved mention is owed to Chiara Brown, who helped me in the translation process of this book, and to Alexandra Buckley from Routledge.

Finally, I must thank Elena and my family. Without them, none of this would have been possible.

Introduction

The right of religious freedom is currently enjoying renewed centrality in scholarly interest, with the emergence of new journals, publications, and research centers and projects.[1] For those observing the developments in the US context, this centrality comes as no surprise. As Elizabeth Shakman Hurd wrote:

> In the United States, religious freedom is often described as the "first freedom", a fundamental human right, a *sine qua non* of modern democratic politics, if not of civilization itself. Americans, we are told, invented and perfected religious freedom. It is ready for export. Today, a rapidly escalating number of international authorities are promoting religious freedom as a foreign policy objective.[2]

This is the starting point for the research discussed in this book. Over the years, the United States has developed institutions and policies aimed at influencing the protection and promotion of religious freedom around the world. A recent increase in the persecution of many religious minorities suggests that these initiatives are probably not always very successful.[3] And yet an increasing number of states and supranational institutions, e.g., the European Union, are also concentrating their efforts on the protection of religious freedom, particularly in relations with other states. Could these developments offer a useful opportunity for reflection in the study of the relationship between law and religion?

First we must address the problem of terminology. The sources used for this book interchangeably use the terms "freedom of religion," "religious freedom," "religious liberty," and "freedom of religion or belief." In the Italian version of this book, I choose to translate all these expressions with the term "libertà religiosa" [religious freedom]. We will see that beyond nominalist disputes, the differences in legal language are an important indication of a growing fragmentation in the notion of religious freedom in the international arena. Despite growing difficulties, according to the Pew Global Attitudes Survey, only 2 percent of the global population believes that religious freedom is *not* fundamental in defining the future aspirations of an individual and collective life plan, such that many constitutional

[1] One might think for instance at the creation of the *Oxford Journal of Law and Religion* or at the relaunch of the *Journal of Law and Religion*, now published by Cambridge University Press.

[2] Elizabeth Shakman Hurd, "Religious Freedom American-style," *Quaderni di Diritto e Politica Ecclesiastica*, no. 1, (2014): p. 231.

[3] Pew Research Center, *Religious Hostilities Reach a Six-Years High*, 14/1/2014, available at: www.pewforum.org/2014/01/14/religious-hostilities-reach-six-year-high/.

texts and international treaties guarantee its protection.[4] Recent studies also reveal a significant correlation between the level of protection of religious freedom and other social benefits.[5] And this was one of the primary motives for scholars – particularly legal scholars – to investigate the role of religious freedom in international and transnational policy and law.

Religion was not initially considered a high-priority element of international policy, and scholars have rediscovered it only over the past twenty years.[6] However, as we shall see, in the case of the United States, it is possible to identify specific historical influences associated with the interpretation of constitutional principles wherein religious freedom plays a key role. The experience in the United States, then, has been fundamental in the establishment of international institutions.[7] After discussing the US experience, particularly the ratification of the International Religious Freedom Act of 1998[8] and its consequences, this book will examine the influence of the US model in the creation of a few fundamental institutions of the European Union and in several countries such as France, Italy, and the United Kingdom. Finally, Part Three will discuss the growing phenomenon of the development, by certain religious groups, of an alternative concept of religious freedom in competition with one that is perceived as being too "Western" and "individualist." The result is a

4 The data are reported by Brian Grim: "To judge from international survey data, people the world over want to be able to practice their religion freely. In the 2007 Pew Global Attitudes Survey, publics in 34 countries covering five different regions were asked about the importance of practicing their religion freely. The response was extremely high, ranging from 84 percent in Eastern Europe to 98 percent in Africa. On average across the 34 countries, they can practice their religion freely, with less than 2 percent indicating that it wasn't important." See Brian J. Grim, "Religious Freedom: Good for What Ails Us?," *Review of Faith and International Affairs* 6, no. 2, (2008): p. 3. For a general survey of religious demography in the world see Brian J. Grim, Todd M. Johnson, Vegard Skirbekk, and Gina A. Zurlo (eds.), *Yearbook of International Religious Demography 2014* (Leiden: Brill, 2014).

5 To substantiate this claim Brian Grim quotes the researches of the Hudson Institute according to which: "[...] wherever religious freedom is high, there tends to be fewer incidents of armed conflicts, better health outcomes, higher level of earned income, and better educational opportunities for women. Moreover religious freedom is associated with higher overall human development, as measured by the human development index." See Brian J. Grim, *Religious Freedom: Good for What Ails Us?*, p. 4. Other scholars, among them Scott Thomas, have highlighted the role of religious freedom and of religious groups in social development. See Scott Thomas, "Faith and Foreign Aid: How the World Bank Got Religion, and Why it Matters," *The Brandywine Review of Faith and International Affairs*, 2, no. 2, (2004): pp. 21–29; see also Brian J. Grim, Greg Clark and Robert E. Snyder, "Is Religious Freedom Good for Business? A Conceptual and Empirical Analysis," *Interdisciplinary Journal of Research on Religion* 10, (2014): pp. 1–18.

6 To this extent it is very interesting to read what Robert Seiple (first US Ambassador for International Religious Freedom) wrote in the first op/ed of the *Brandywine Review of Faith and International Affairs* which, some years later, became *The Review of Faith and International Affairs*: "A survey of some 1600 articles in four leading International relations journals over the period 1980–1999 finds only a handful featuring religion as an important influence. [...] since the late 1990s however, a number of factors have converged to begin raising the profile of religion in international affairs." See Robert A. Seiple, "Why Brandywine Review?" *The Brandywine Review of Faith and International Affairs* 1, no. 1, (2003): p. 1. For an introduction to the topic see Daniel Philpott, "Has the Study of Global Politics Found Religion?" *The Annual Review of Political Science* 12, (2009): pp. 183–202 and also Olivier Roy, "Religious revivals as a product and tool of globalization," *Quaderni di Relazioni Internationali* 12, no. 2, (2010): pp. 22–34.

7 For an introduction to the topic see Gregorio Bettiza, "Religion and American Foreign Policy in the Context of the Post-secular Turn in World Politics and Social Sciences," *International Politics Review* 1, no. 1, (2013): pp. 11–26 while for an approach more focused on legal developments see Anna L. Su, *Exporting Freedom: Religious Liberty and American Power* (Cambridge: Harvard University Press, 2016).

8 US Congress, *International Religious Freedom Act of 1998*, Public Law 105–292, H.R. 2431, 27/8/1998.

religious freedom that is often weak in its universal and unitarian aspects, and threatened by specific political and national interests. This, however, is not necessarily reason to abandon the concept of religious freedom, as not only a fundamental right, but as a desire for individual and collective emancipation.

References

Bettiza, Gregorio, "Religion and American Foreign Policy in the Context of the Post-secular Turn in World Politics and Social Sciences," *International Politics Review* 1, no. 1, (2013): pp. 11–26.

Grim, Brian J., Johnson, Todd M., Skirbekk, Vegard, and Zurlo, Gina A. (eds.), *Yearbook of International Religious Demography 2014* (Leiden: Brill, 2014).

Grim, Brian J., Clark, Greg, and Snyder, Robert E., "Is Religious Freedom Good for Business? A Conceptual and Empirical Analysis," *Interdisciplinary Journal of Research on Religion* 10, (2014): pp. 1–18.

Grim, Brian J., "Religious Freedom: Good for What Ails Us?," *Review of Faith and International Affairs* 6, no. 2, (2008): pp. 3–7.

Pew Research Center, *Religious Hostilities Reach a Six-Years High*, 14/1/2014, available at: www.pewforum.org/2014/01/14/religious-hostilities-reach-six-year-high/

Philpott, Daniel, "Has the Study of Global Politics Found Religion?," *The Annual Review of Political Science* 12, (2009): pp. 183–202.

Roy, Olivier, "Religious revivals as a product and tool of globalization," *Quaderni di Relazioni Internazionali* 12, no. 2, (2010): pp. 22–34.

Seiple, Robert A., "Why Brandywine Review?," *The Brandywine Review of Faith and International Affairs* 1, no. 1, (2003): pp. 1–2.

Shakman Hurd, Elizabeth, "Religious Freedom American-style," *Quaderni di Diritto e Politica Ecclesiastica*, no. 1, (2014): pp. 231–242.

Su, Anna L., *Exporting Freedom: Religious Liberty and American Power* (Cambridge: Harvard University Press, 2016).

Thomas, Scott, "Faith and Foreign Aid: How the World Bank Got Religion, and Why it Matters," *The Brandywine Review of Faith and International Affairs*, 2, no. 2, (2004): pp. 21–29.

Part I

The United States and the International Religious Freedom Act

1 The first freedom

1. A "shining city upon a hill": American exceptionalism and religious freedom

In the American political imagination, there is a recurring image of a shining city on a hill, a city that could give rise to a new political order, replacing European violence with a new system of co-existence among people of different religious faiths. This vision is often associated with the narrative of the uniqueness and exceptionality of America in world history.[1]

For more than 400 years, this exceptionalism has been one of the fundamental characteristics of the American narrative: the uniqueness of the historic events that gave rise to the birth of the United States of America and which, in the analysis of some authors, assigned to it a special position and mission in the world.[2] This idea of the "differentness" of the United States is also reflected in its relationships with its peers; hence where in Europe nationality is related with *community*, the principal carrier of identity in the United States is often *ideology*. As Seymour Martin Lipset observes: "In Europe, nationality is related to community, and thus one cannot become un-English or un-Swedish. Being an American, however, is an ideological commitment. It is not a matter of birth. Those who reject American values are un-American."[3]

Jack Greene reminds us that in fact the genesis of American exceptionalism can be found in medieval Europe, which imagined a place that could redeem the sins and vices of the Old World (Europe), which had been corrupted and which was by then beyond redemption.[4]

1 When the names of the American Founding Founders are listed an often forgotten name is John Winthrop which, instead, can be listed as one of the intellectual points of reference for what may concern the idea that the United States have of themselves and aspire to project in the world. On John Winthrop see Francis J. Bremer, *John Winthrop: America's Forgotten Founding Father* (Oxford: Oxford University Press, 2003). For a critical opinion on Winthrop's thought see Mark A. Noll, "'We Shall Be as a City upon a Hill': John Winthrop's Non-American Exceptionalism," *The Review of Faith and International Affairs*, 10, no. 2, 2012, pp. 5–11.

2 See Deborah L. Madsen, *American Exceptionalism* (Jackson: Mississippi University Press, 1998) and Chris Seiple, "The Essence of Exceptionalism: Roger Williams and the Birth of Religious Freedom in America," *The Review of Faith and International Affairs*, 10, no. 2, 2012, pp. 13–19.

3 Seymour M. Lipset, *American Exceptionalism: A Double Edged Sword* (New York: W.W. Norton & Company, 1996), p. 31.

4 As Jack Greene argues: "Throughout the Middle Ages, Europeans had posited the existence of a place for a time to the east, but mostly to the West of Europe without the corruptions and disadvantages of the Old World. The discovery of America merely intensified this 'nostalgia for the Golden Age and Lost Paradise' and actually aroused new hope for their discovery somewhere on the western edge of the Atlantic." See Jack Greene, *The Intellectual Construction of America. Exceptionalism and Identity from 1942 to 1800* (Chapel Hill: University of North Carolina Press, 1993), pp. 25–26.

Many historical events, therefore, can be used to trace back the origins of the founding of the United States. The mission of the first Puritans who landed in New England was to create a new Church and a new society capable of saving a humanity (Europe) that had fallen into disgrace. As Deborah Madsen points out:

> In this view, the New World is the last and best chance offered by God to a fallen humanity that has only to look to His exceptional new church for redemption. Thus, America and Americans are special, exceptional, because they are charged with saving the world from itself and, at the same time, America and Americans must sustain a high level of spiritual, political and moral commitment to this exceptional destiny – America must be as "a city upon a hill" exposed to the eyes of the world.[5]

As noted by Steven Calabresi, many references to the "new world" and the "city upon a hill" are actually reinterpretations of biblical passages, particularly from the book of Matthew.[6] Over the years, rapid social and political changes have led to the emergence and addition of more secular narratives.[7] American exceptionalism – as with political moralism applied to foreign policy – has thus become a constant in the history of the United States. From the war on communist regimes to the countries of the "axis of evil" named by George W. Bush, its use – at times, its exploitation – as justification for US interventions in other countries has multiplied. And these claims are not seen only in the documents or speeches of Republican presidents: in his first inaugural address, John F. Kennedy himself neatly summarized the characteristics of American exceptionalism – the appeal to God on the one hand, and the desire to rise up to be a model for other countries on the other, being tasked with a mission of almost divine origin:

> I have sworn before you and Almighty God the same solemn oath our forebears prescribed nearly a century and three quarters ago [...] Let every nation know, whether it wishes us well or ill, that we shall pay any price, bear any burden, meet any hardship, support any friend, oppose any foe to assure the survival and the success of liberty.[8]

5 See Deborah L. Madsen, *American Exceptionalism*, pp. 1–2. The metaphor of the "city upon a hill" is taken from a sermon that John Winthrop made in 1630 title "*A Model of Christian Charity*" in which he said: "For we must consider that we shall be a city upon a hill. The eyes of all people are upon us. So that if we shall deal falsely with our God in this work we have undertaken, and so cause him to withdraw his present help from us, we shall be made a story and by-word through the world." Quoted in Steven Calabresi, "'A Shining City on a Hill': American Exceptionalism and the Supreme Court's Practice of Relying on Foreign Law," *Boston University Law Review* 86, (2006): p. 1336.

6 Steven Calabresi, "'A Shining City on a Hill': American Exceptionalism and the Supreme Court's Practice of Relying on Foreign Law," p. 1348.

7 On this point Steven Calabresi mentions the position of Deborah Madsen which connects the secularist culture of Benjamin Franklin to a new dimension of American exceptionalism: "Franklin powerfully redefined the Puritan mission: recasting the terms of success, where material prosperity assumed a prominence it had not had before, where the conditions of life for Americans were defined less in spiritual terms than earlier, where the collective salvation of the community was transformed into a form of government that would protect the rights of all citizens. What remained was the perception that America would continue to be judged by the other nations of the world to whom America would remain a model, a guide, a measure. And also a guardian of inalienable rights of man, so recently enshrined in the Constitution." *Ibid.*, p. 1354.

8 John F. Kennedy, *Inaugural Address*, 20/1/1961, available at: www.jfklibrary.org. It has also been argued that "Americanism" might be a religion in itself. See David Gelernter, *Americanism: The Fourth Great Western Religion* (New York: Doubleday, 2007).

This theme was repeatedly invoked by Ronald Reagan as well, who was perhaps the president who most often used the metaphor of the "shining city on a hill."[9] Thus this exceptionalism has remained a constant in US political development since the colonists first arrived in New England.[10] This pre-political element deeply informs the United States' projection of itself and its institutions into the world, and remains an emblematic element of what it means to be US citizens.

The meeting point of the various influences of exceptionalism can be found in the text of the US Constitution which, in Steven Calabresi's analysis, is the tangible political and legal result of this narrative. It touches precisely on the First Amendment to the Constitution, which also guarantees religious freedom,[11] giving it a central position of importance in the promotion of the "politics of liberty" which is typical of the way that the United States – among the various revolutions that distinguish the history of the West, starting with the English Revolution – confronts modernity.[12] The first amendment to the US Constitution is the result of a lengthy historical process of rejecting the experience of the State Church and the religious persecution that many of the founding fathers had experienced in Europe. In this sense, according to the traditional narrative, the primary objective of this provision was to create the first "marketplace of religions," for the truly equal treatment of all religious faiths, whose sustenance and vigor would have depended solely on the commitment of the faithful, and not the assistance of public powers.[13] In reality, the history of religious freedom in the United States has demonstrated how easily the persecuted can become the persecutors, and how secular powers and public institutions can be used to build a new State Church.[14] The political and legal journey to full religious freedom is long, even in the United States. It is a journey that continues even today.

2. "First freedom": The United States and religious freedom

In 1948, after long negotiations, Article 18 of the Universal Declaration of Human Rights of the United Nations was approved, ensuring freedom of thought, conscience, and

9 Steven Calabresi lists numerous occasions, among them a famous speech by Ronald Reagan in 1974: "We cannot escape our destiny nor should we try to do so. The leadership of the free world was thrust upon us two centuries ago in that little hall in Philadelphia. In the days following World War II, when the economic strength and power of America was all that stood between the world and the return to the dark ages, Pope Pius XII said 'the American people have a great genius for splendid and unselfish actions. Into the hands of America God has placed the destinies of an afflicted mankind'. We are indeed, and we are today, the last best hope of man on earth," Governor Ronald Reagan, Remarks at the Conservative Political Action Conference, 25/1/1974 quoted in Steven Calabresi, "'A Shining City on a Hill': American Exceptionalism and the Supreme Court's Practice of Relying on Foreign Law," p. 1371.

10 For an analysis of the influence of religious ideas on American exceptionalism see James L. Guth, "The Religious Roots of Foreign Policy Exceptionalism," *The Review of Faith and International Affairs*, 10, no. 2, (2012): pp. 77–85.

11 According to the First Amendment to the US Constitution: "Congress shall make no law respecting an establishment of religion, or prohibiting the free exercise thereof; or abridging the freedom of speech, or of the press; or of the right of the people peaceably to assemble, and to petition the government for a redress of grievances."

12 Gertrude Himmelfarb, *The Roads to Modernity: The British, French and American Enlightenments* (New York: Vintage Books, 2004).

13 See Allen D. Hertzke, International Religious Freedom Policy: Taking Stock, *The Review of Faith and International Affairs* 6, no. 2, (2008): pp. 17–23.

14 See David Sehat, *The Myth of American Religious Freedom* (New York: Oxford University Press, 2011).

religion.[15] In 1966, the governments of 167 countries signed the International Treaty on Civil and Political Rights, which also ensures freedom of religion and conscience. In 1981, the Declaration on the Elimination of All Forms of Intolerance and of Discrimination Based on Religion or Belief was approved. During this period, the United Nations entered into multiple agreements on the protection of religious freedom. According to Samuel Moyn, the centrality of religious freedom in the history of charters and declarations of human rights can be traced back to the particular period in which these documents were approved. In the case of the Universal Declaration of Human Rights, the insistence on the importance of Article 18 is related to the battle against communist regimes and their policies of state atheism and persecution based on religion and of religious minorities. These policies created a backlash from some American Christian communities, who saw the battle against the atheistic Communist regime as a battle of civilizations in the defense of religion and religious freedom, which was also to be fought through the use of supranational institutions.[16] The religious freedom of the West, then, was a bulwark against the threat of Communist atheism.

Samuel Moyn reflects on its nodal importance in understanding the genesis and mutation of the concept of religious freedom as expressed in the documents of international law, and shows how the US model has played a central role in the internationalization of policies on religious freedom, including within multilateral bodies.

Before considering this perspective, however, it seems appropriate to provide a brief overview of the position of religious freedom within the US legal system, the instruments available for its protection, and its legislative and jurisprudential developments. Starting with the internal dynamics of the United States will help us understand how, over the past several years, religious freedom has become the subject of policies that are increasingly coordinated between different states, becoming a central basis for their foreign policy actions.

The Constitution of 1789 contains no explicit, specific provision regulating relations between Church and State. The only article in the Constitution that explicitly mentions religion is, in fact, Article VI, where it prohibits religious tests or declarations of faith as a condition for taking public office. It was only in 1791 with the approval of the Bill of Rights that the United States became equipped with a catalog of fundamental rights guaranteed to citizens, limiting the action of the state and helping to create a jurisprudence on the protection of fundamental rights which has inspired the legislation of many countries

15 According to article 18 of the Universal Declaration of Human Rights: "Everyone has the right to freedom of thought, conscience and religion; this right includes freedom to change his religion or belief, and freedom, either alone or in community with others and in public or private, to manifest his religion or belief in teaching, practice, worship and observance." See Linde Lindkvist, *Religious Freedom and the Universal Declaration of Human Rights* (Cambridge: Cambridge University Press, 2017).

16 Samuel Moyn mentions in particular the different protestant groups and denominations and their reactions to the internationalist project advanced by President Franklin Delano Roosevelt: "During the war, when the idea of 'human rights' began to circulate for the first time in the English language, American mainline Protestants responded to Franklin Delano Roosevelt's Four Freedom promises (the second of which offered freedom of religion everywhere in the world) by making human rights central to international activism for the first time in history. [...] These American Protestants put aside their internal disputes about whether Christianity demanded pacifism (and staying out of the European war). After the war's end, they were by any standard most responsible for the original move to internationalize religious freedom, and in fact for the presence of the entire notion of human rights in international affairs." See Samuel Moyn, "From Communist to Muslims: European Human Rights, the Cold War, and Religious Liberty," *South Atlantic Quarterly* 113, no. 1, (2014): p. 68.

throughout the world. The First Amendment to the Constitution is of particular interest for the purposes of our analysis, since in addition to protecting religious freedom, it also protects freedom of expression, freedom of speech, and the right of citizens to assemble peacefully and petition the government. With regard to religious freedom, under the First Amendment: "Congress shall make no law respecting an establishment of religion, or prohibiting the free exercise thereof."

The First Amendment is made up of two clauses: the Free Exercise clause, and the Establishment Clause, both aimed at protecting part of the doctrine defined as "First Freedom," or the right of religious freedom.[17] As John Witte Jr. and Joel Nichols have pointed out, multiple political and theological frameworks and influences led to the approval of the First Amendment[18]; furthermore, this same religious pluralism has played a major role in the level of pluralism of the United States experience.[19] On the one hand, it has been demonstrated that religious groups themselves felt the need for a distinction and potential separation between the state and themselves[20]; and on the other hand, the

17 See Michael W. McConnell, "Why is Religious Liberty the 'First Freedom'?" *Cardozo Law Review*, 21, (1999–2000): pp. 1243–1265. From an historical point of view, and taking into account the different positions of the constitutional amendments, McConnell highlights how the fact that the right to religious freedom is part of the first amendment is not to be considered a simple "accident": "As a historical proposition, the answer to this question is simple. it was an accident. If Madison, the principal architect of the Bill of Rights, had had his way, a Religious Clause would have been tucked away somewhere between Clauses 3 and 4 of Article I, Section 9. On this point, as on so many, Madison gave way to his colleagues, who preferred a separate set of amendments." *Ibid.*, p. 1243. According to McConnell at the right to religious liberty needs to be recognized as a substantial historical and philosophical relevance: "Long before liberalism was conceived in theory or in practice, the division between temporal and spiritual authority gave rise to the most fundamental features of liberal democratic order: the idea of limited government, the idea of individual conscience and hence individual rights, and the idea of a civil society, as apart from government, bearing primary responsibility for the formation and transmission of opinions and ideas. These ideas came about not in rebellion against religion, but in defence of religion against the encroachment of the state." *Ibid.*, p. 1244.

18 John Witte Jr., Joel A. Nichols, *Religion and the American Constitutional Experiment* (Boulder: Westview, 2010).

19 This point is highlighted by Noah Feldman: "The political reasons for the clauses was that no one in the new United States opposed the idea of religious liberty, and given the religious diversity among Americans, no one denomination seriously believed it could establish a national religion of its own. Although 95 percent were Protestants of some sort (as of 1780 there were just fifty-six Catholic churches and five Jewish congregations in the whole country), American Protestants ranged from Anglican (soon to be renamed Episcopalian) and Congregationalist to Presbyterian, Baptist, Quaker, and beyond. Practically speaking, the fact of religious diversity made a nationally established religion impossible." See Noah Feldman, *Divided by God: America's Church and State Problem and What We Should Do About It* (New York: Farrar, Straus & Giroux, 2005), p. 20.

20 This is an aspect highlighted by Michael McConnell: "The drive for religious freedom was part of this evangelical movement. It is anachronistic to assume, based on modern patterns, that governmental aid to religion and suppression of heterodoxy were opposed by the more rationalistic and supported by the more intense religious believers of that era. The most intense religious sects opposed establishment on the ground that it injured religion and subjected it to the control of civil authorities. Guaranteed state support was thought to stifle religious enthusiasm and initiative. [...] The newer, more enthusiastic sects had the most to gain from breaking the monopoly of the established church. [...] The greatest support for disestablishment and free exercise therefore came from evangelical Protestant denominations, especially Baptists and Quakers, but also from Presbyterians." See Michael W. McConnell, "The Origins and Historical Understanding of Free Exercise of Religion," *Harvard Law Review* 103, no. 7, (1990): pp. 1438–1439.

influence of the thought of Thomas Jefferson,[21] James Madison, and John Locke[22] are certainly worthy of mention.

It should be pointed out that it was only starting in the 1940s, through the interpretative powers of the Supreme Court, that the two constitutional clauses ended up being applied not only to Congress, but also to the states.[23] Despite the fundamental role of the Supreme Court, it should be noted that it exists within a system where the standard of protection provided by the federal system exists side-by-side with the system of protection of religious freedom provided by the various states through the state constitutions and specific Bills of Rights.

In the overall development of the protection of religious freedom in the United States, which is impossible to fully describe here, the Supreme Court Decision *Employment Division vs. Smith*[24] deserves particular attention. This case was the appeal of a federal law prohibiting the use of peyote and other hallucinogenic drugs used by Native Americans during their religious ceremonies. The State of Oregon denied unemployment benefits to two Indians (Smith and Black) who were fired for the illegal use of hallucinogenic substances during the religious rituals of the Native American Church. After a long and complex judicial process, the Supreme Court, with an opinion by Justice Scalia, held that the wording of the law was general in nature and not directed against a specific religious group. Based on this argument, it overturned the decision in the previous case, *Sherbert vs. Verner*,[25] ruling that the primary purpose of the law was not to directly penalize a religious rite, but affected it only incidentally, and so should be considered legitimate with respect to the Free Exercise Clause of the First Amendment to the Constitution.[26]

21 For an analysis of Jefferson's role see Daniel L. Dreisbach, *Thomas Jefferson and the Wall of Separation Between Church and State* (New York: New York University Press, 2002). For a critical approach see Mark J. Chadsey, "Thomas Jefferson and the Establishment Clause," *Akron Law Review* 40, (2007): pp. 623–646. Also Feldman raises some issues on Jefferson's role: "The problem with this emphasis on Jefferson's role in the shaping of religious liberty in America is that although he did write the Virginia statute, he was in Paris as the American ambassador in 1786 when the Bill of Rights including the First Amendment was added to the Constitution. Indeed Jefferson missed the entire Constitutional Convention." See Noah Feldman, *Divided by God: America's Church and State Problem and What We Should Do About It*, p. 24.

22 *See* Noah Feldman, "The Intellectual Origins of the Establishment Clause," *New York University Law Review* 77, (2002): pp. 346–428.

23 In *Cantwell v. Connecticut*, for the first time, the US Supreme Court applied the Free Exercise Clause of the first amendment against a local ordinance. In 1947 in *Everson v. Board of Education* the Supreme Court applied the Establishment Clause to the States. According to Justice Black: "The meaning and scope of the First Amendment, preventing an establishment of religion or prohibiting the free exercise thereof, in light of its history and the evils it was designed forever to suppress, have been several times elaborated by the decisions of this Court prior to the application of the First Amendment to the states by the Fourteenth. The broad meaning given to the Amendment by these earlier cases has been accepted by this Court in its decisions concerning an individual's religious freedom (of exercise) [...] There is every reason to give the same application and broad interpretation to the 'establishment of religion' clause." See *Everson v. Board of Education*, 330 U.S. 1, 1947, 14–15.

24 *Employment Division v. Smith*, 494 U.S. 872, 1990.

25 *Sherbert v. Verner*, 374 U.S. 398, 1963.

26 To use the words of the Supreme Court: "An individual's religious beliefs do not excuse him from compliance with an otherwise valid law prohibiting conduct that the State is free to regulate." See *Employment Division v. Smith*, 878–879. The decision authored by Justice Scalia privileges the protection of religious interests through the political process rather than through the judiciary: "It may be fairly be said that leaving accommodation to the political process will place at a relative disadvantage those religious practices that are not widely engaged in; but that unavoidable consequence of democratic government must be preferred to a system in which each conscience is a law unto itself or in which judges weigh the social importance of all laws against the centrality of all religious beliefs," 890.

This decision deeply affected the principle of individual religious freedom, endorsing the application of laws of general scope and the authority of the state with respect to potential religiously motivated demands. As Francesco Onida points out: "Now a general law always prevails over religious behavior: 'only' the balancing test, applicable 'only' to cases of unemployment compensation, can provoke a rare exception."[27]

The approach of the Supreme Court[28] in the *Smith* case therefore tended to transform the right of religious freedom into the right of formal equality of citizens before the law.[29] The Court's decision with the *Smith* ruling, which subordinated the protection of the principle of individual religious freedom to the needs of general legislation, gave rise to a bitter conflict between judicial power and legislative power aimed at restoring the protection of the principle of religious freedom as understood prior to the *Smith* case through the introduction of the Religious Freedom Restoration Act.[30] This measure, which became law on November 16, 1993, was aimed at preventing limitation of the individual's right of religious freedom, including through neutral and general laws, unless such laws are justified by a compelling state interest, and are proportional to its stated aim. However, just three years later, in the case of the *City of Boerne vs. Flores*,[31] the Supreme Court ruled this legislative act partially unconstitutional and revived the decision in the *Smith* case, imposing severe limits on the potential extension of the protection provided by legislative power.[32] The standard of protection intended with the Religious Freedom Restoration Act still applies only to federal legislation, not state legislation, which is therefore evaluated according to more stringent criteria.[33] For example, early in the tenure of Chief Justice

[27] See Francesco Onida, "Stati Uniti d'America. Clausole religiose del primo emendamento del Bill of Rights, free exercise ed establishment della religione, controversie religiose e competenza del giudice statuale," in Francesco Margiotta Broglio, Cesare Mirabelli, Francesco Onida (eds.), *Religioni e sistemi giuridici. Introduzione al diritto ecclesiastico comparato* (Bologna: Il Mulino, 2004), p. 296.

[28] An anticipation of this approach can be seen in *Goldman v. Weinberger* in which the Supreme Court said that a Jewish doctor didn't have the right to wear the kippah during working hours. See *Goldman v. Weinberger*, 475 U.S. 503, 1986.

[29] On this point the thought of Frederick Gedicks is illuminating: "Freedom of religion after Smith is less a liberty right than an equality right. To say that the Free Exercise Clause protects only against government action that intentionally burdens religious liberty, as Smith does, means that in terms of 'limitations', the law in the United States is that religious activity generally may be limited for any reason other than antireligious animus." See Frederick M. Gedicks, "Religious Exemptions, Formal Neutrality and Laïcité," *Indiana Journal of Global Legal Studies* 13, (2006): p. 478.

[30] US Congress, *Religious Freedom Restoration Act*, Public Law 103–141. 16/11/1993.

[31] *City of Boerne v. Flores*, 521 U.S. 507, 1997.

[32] The contrast between the judiciary and the legislative power, with the prevalence of the first, has been highlighted by John Noonan according to which in *City of Boerne v. Flores*: "[...] the intervention of Congress in a fight within the Court is treated as lèse majesté, and Congress bluntly told to butt out." See John T. Noonan jr., "The First Freedom and the Rehnquist Court," in Martin H. Belsky (eds.), *The Rehnquist Court. A Retrospective* (Oxford: Oxford University Press, 2002), p. 76.

[33] It is worth mentioning another law that was passed by Congress in order to guarantee a more robust protection of religious freedom: the *Religious Land Use and Institutionalized Person Act* which imposes the strict scrutiny test to assess zoning laws and the right of inmates. See the Supreme Court decision *Cutter v. Wilkinson*, 544 U.S. 709, 2005 and also Douglas Laycock, "RFRA, Congress and the Ratchet," *Montana Law Review* 56, (1995): pp. 145–170. The Religious Freedom Restoration Act has been key to a landmark US Supreme Court decision in 2014 in the case *Burweel, Secretary of Health and Human Services et al. v. Hobby Lobby Stores Inc. et al. and Conestoga Wood Specialities Corp et al. v. Burwell, Secretary of Health and Human Services et al.*, 573 U.S. 2014. For the Supreme Court the request of the federal government according to which employer, with the exception of non-profit companies, should cover health insurance of the employees and also their contraceptives, is not compatible with the

Roberts,[34] in *Gonzalez vs. O'Centro Espirita Beneficiente Uniao Do Vegetal*,[35] the Court unanimously declared incompatible with the Religious Freedom Restoration Act federal legislation prohibiting the import of a hallucinogenic herb used for the rituals of a certain religious denomination.

It can be said, however, that with this last decision, Supreme Court jurisprudence on the protection of religious freedom – despite all the precautions this topic requires, and taking into account the multiple levels of protection offered by the US legal system – cleared the way for greater protection of religious freedom compared to what was theorized in the early 1990s with the decision in the *Smith* case. However, this protection appears to be entrusted more to state and federal laws and various state constitutions than to Supreme Court jurisprudence.[36] The decision in the *Smith* case played a decisive role in the developments related to our topic. Many religious groups have seen their religious freedom threatened by a ruling that does not guarantee exemptions from general law, and sees religious freedom no longer as a "special" freedom but as a mere right to equal treatment before the law. As Winnifred Sullivan maintains, the Supreme Court decision was fundamental, invoking a political reaction significant enough to push Congress to approve measures to overturn the outcome and result of the Court's ruling.

The *Smith* case therefore profoundly changed the perception of protection of the interests of religious groups and the debate on religious freedom in the United States, both from the perspective of domestic law and international projection, incentivizing the formation of a heretofore unheard of political alliance among various religious groups to protect the benefits guaranteed to them under the US legal system. The role of religious freedom in US foreign policy, however, has very old roots, which we must briefly touch on before analyzing the regulatory measures approved by the US Congress in the second half of the 1990s, which made the promotion of religious freedom a priority of the US government.

3. Religious freedom in United States foreign policy

The contribution of the United States to the history and development of the protection of religious freedom is certainly unique.[37] It would be impossible to understand its historical

Religious Freedom Restoration Act. See also Paul Horwitz, "The Hobby Lobby Moment," *Harvard Law Review* 128, no. 1, (2014): pp. 154–189.

34 See Pasquale Annicchino (ed.), *La Corte Roberts e il diritto di libertà religiosa* (Fiesole: EUI University Press, 2017).

35 *Gonzalez v. O'Centro Espirita Beneficiente Uniao Do Vegetal*, 546 U.S. 418, 2006.

36 This is for instance the conclusion reached by Kent Greenawalt: "[...] the significance of the federal Free Exercise Clause has been much diminished, but not eliminated by the Supreme Court's decision in Employment Division v. Smith [...] special protection of free exercise now rest substantially on federal and state statutes, on judicial interpretations of state constitutions and, to a lesser extent, on judicial development of common law." See K. Greenawalt, *Religion and the Constitution. Free Exercise and Fairness*, (Princeton: Princeton University Press, 2009), p. 440. Greenawalt also underlined how: "Smith concerns the allocation of responsibilities between courts and legislatures for creating exemptions from general laws; it does not undercut the appropriateness of legislative exemptions or address the fairness of particular kind of organizations. The opinion makes clear that a legislature may exempt members of the Native American Church from a ban on using peyote, and many state legislatures, including Oregon's have adopted exemptions following Smith." *Ibid.*, p. 155.

37 See Anna L. Su., *Exporting Freedom: Religious Liberty and American Power* (Cambridge: Harvard University Press, 2016).

development, political problems, and intellectual debates apart from the role of religion in US society, and the contributions made by various social groups which, over time, have found a place in the complex political and social mosaic of the United States. At the same time, it would be impossible to understand certain figures – such as Thomas Jefferson, George Washington, James Madison, or John Jay – and their contributions without discussing their positions with regard to religion and religious freedom. According to Andrew Preston, it is precisely because of this centrality of religion in the political development of the US that the First Amendment governs and guarantees the fundamental right of religious freedom:

> The importance with which the Founders viewed religious liberty as a foundational right is one of the main reasons why the Bill of Rights, one of the world's first systematic codification of individual rights, begins with religious freedom (in the Establishment and Free Exercise clauses) before all other rights.[38]

This fundamental aspect can also be seen in the history of US foreign policy: in fact, often the absence of religious freedom is seen by the United States as a sign of a lack of freedom in general, and the possible existence of a tyrannical regime.[39] There is one aspect of Andrew Preston's analysis that may be more useful than any other in explaining the practically messianic centrality of religious freedom in the context of US foreign policy. According to Preston, this event is Franklin Delano Roosevelt's decision to enter into the war against Nazi Germany. In his speech, Roosevelt explicitly refers to the importance of religion as the basis for democratic institutions, international security, and the United States, as well as religious freedom as the foundation of the US political project:

> Where freedom of religion has been attacked, the attack has come from sources opposed to democracy. Where democracy has been overthrown, the spirit of free worship has disappeared. And where religion and democracy have vanished, good faith and reason in international affairs have given way to strident ambition and brute force [...] There comes a time in the affairs of men when they must prepare to defend, not their homes alone, but the tenets of faith and humanity on which their churches, their governments and their very civilization are founded. The defense of religion, of democracy and of good faith among nations is all the same fight. To save one we must now make up our minds to save all. We know what might happen to us of the United States if the new philosophies of force were to encompass the other continents and invade our own. We,

38 Andrew Preston, "The First Human Right: Religious Liberty and the American Diplomatic Tradition," *The Review of Faith and International Affairs*, 11, n. 1, (2013): p. 10. See also Andrew Preston, *Sword of the Spirit, Shield of Faith. Religion in American War and Diplomacy* (New York-Toronto: Knopf, 2012).

39 As argued by Andrew Preston: "[...] many U.S. foreign policy makers have perceived the absence of religious liberty in foreign countries as a primary indicator of tyranny and a warning sign that such countries will behave aggressively." Preston also makes some concrete examples: "This is why Secretary of State Daniel Webster promised to guarantee the safety of Protestant missionaries in Asia and the Pacific in the 1840s and 1850s; it was why Secretary John Jay extended official protection to harassed and beleaguered Protestant missionaries in South America and Mormon missionaries in Europe in the 1890s; and it was why President Theodore Roosevelt and Woodrow Wilson made the status of persecuted Jews in Russia, Romania and Poland a priority for U.S. foreign policy." See Andrew Preston, "The First Human Right: Religious Liberty and the American Diplomatic Tradition," p. 11.

no more than other nations, can afford to be surrounded by the enemies of our faith and our humanity.[40]

Naturally, as Andrew Preston himself admits, it would be incorrect to attribute Franklin Delano Roosevelt's decision to intervene in Europe during the Second World War solely to the religious factor. What is clear, however, is the centrality of human rights in President Roosevelt's foreign policy,[41] and specifically the right of religious freedom. In fact, both the religious rhetoric that formed part of the narrative of his foreign policy and the radical conviction that fundamental rights could be the basis for a new global order would lead Franklin Delano Roosevelt to play a major role in the post-World War II political process which led to the approval of the Universal Declaration of Human Rights at the United Nations.[42] Roosevelt also stated that one of the political objectives of Nazism was to eliminate all religions:

> [...] abolish all existing religions: Catholic, Protestant, Mohammedan, Buddhist, Hindu, and Jewish alike and in the place of the churches of our civilization, there is to be set up an International Nazi Church staffed with orators of the Nazi regime.[43]

Religious references can also be found in the foreign policy speeches and statements of other US presidents. Ronald Reagan made ample use of religious rhetoric, often highlighting the need to protect religious freedom, which was repeatedly violated in Communist countries and in the former Soviet Union. After 1989, George H.W. Bush, Bill Clinton, George W. Bush, and Barack Obama often made reference to the importance of religious freedom. However, to understand the origins and developments of US legislation aimed at making religious freedom one of the fundamental principles of its foreign policy, we must look back to anti-Communism, and the fight against the Communist political regime which characterized the domestic and foreign policy of the United States for many years.[44]

40 Franklin Delano Roosevelt, *State of the Union Address*, 4/1/1939, available at: www.infoplease.com/t/hist/state-of-the-union/150.html.

41 It is also worth reminding that President Roosevelt appointed a personal representative to the Holy See. See George Q. Flynn, "Franklin Roosevelt and the Vatican: The Myron Taylor Appointment to the Vatican," *Catholic Historical Review*, 58, n. 2, (1972): pp. 171–194.

42 The reference to religious freedom is already present from 1942: "Subsequently, the Roosevelt administration followed through on the president's rhetorical flourishes by including religious freedom in the war's key diplomatic texts such as the United Nation Declaration of January 1942 and the founding charter of the UN, signed in San Francisco in 1945." See Andrew Preston, "The First Human Right: Religious Liberty and the American Diplomatic Tradition," p. 12. As Anna Su has shown also Woodrow Wilson made several attempts to focus the action of supranational institutions on religious freedom. See Anna L. Su, "Woodrow Wilson and the Origins of the International Law of Religious Freedom," *Journal of History of International Law*, 15, (2013): pp. 235–267.

43 Samuel Rosenman, *Working with Roosevelt* (New York: Harper & Brothers, 1952), p. 195.

44 See Jeremy Gunn, *Spiritual Weapons: The Cold War and the Forging of an American National Religion* (Westport: Praeger, 2008) and also Jonathan P. Herzog, *The Spiritual-Industrial Complex: America's Religious Battle against Communism in the Early Cold War* (New York: Oxford University Press, 2011).

References

Annicchino, Pasquale (ed.), *La Corte Roberts e il diritto di libertà religiosa* (Fiesole: EUI University Press, 2017).

Bremer, Francis J., *John Winthrop: America's Forgotten Founding Father* (Oxford: Oxford University Press, 2003).

Calabresi, Steven, "'A Shining City on a Hill': American Exceptionalism and the Supreme Court's Practice of Relying on Foreign Law," *Boston University Law Review* 86, (2006): pp. 1335–1416.

Chadsey, Mark J., "Thomas Jefferson and the Establishment Clause," *Akron Law Review* 40, (2007): pp. 623–646.

Delano Roosevelt, Franklin, *State of the Union Address*, 4/1/1939, available at: www.infoplease.com/t/hist/state-of-the-union/150.html

Dreisbach, Daniel L., *Thomas Jefferson and the Wall of Separation Between Church and State* (New York: New York University Press, 2002).

Feldman, Noah, *Divided by God: America's Church and State Problem and What We Should Do About It* (New York: Farrar, Straus & Giroux, 2005).

Feldman, Noah, "The Intellectual Origins of the Establishment Clause," *New York University Law Review* 77, (2002): pp. 346–428.

Flynn, George Q., "Franklin Roosevelt and the Vatican: The Myron Taylor Appointment to the Vatican," *Catholic Historical Review*, 58, n. 2, (1972): pp. 171–194.

Gelernter, David, *Americanism: The Fourth Great Western Religion* (New York: Doubleday, 2007).

Gedicks, Frederick M., "Religious Exemptions, Formal Neutrality and Laïcité", *Indiana Journal of Global Legal Studies* 13, (2006): pp. 473–492.

Greene, Jack, *The Intellectual Construction of America. Exceptionalism and Identity from 1942 to 1800* (Chapel Hill: University of North Carolina Press, 1993).

Gunn, Jeremy, *Spiritual Weapons: The Cold War and the Forging of an American National Religion* (Westport: Praeger, 2008).

Guth, James L., "The Religious Roots of Foreign Policy Exceptionalism," *The Review of Faith and International Affairs*, 10, no. 2, (2012): pp. 77–85.

Hertzke, Allen D., "International Religious Freedom Policy: Taking Stock," *The Review of Faith and International Affairs* 6, no. 2, (2008): pp. 17–23.

Herzog, Jonathan P., *The Spiritual-Industrial Complex: America's Religious Battle against Communism in the Early Cold War* (New York: Oxford University Press, 2011).

Himmelfarb, Gertrude, *The Roads to Modernity: The British, French and American Enlightenments* (New York: Vintage Books, 2004).

Kennedy, John F., *Inaugural Address*, 20/1/1961, available at: www.jfklibrary.org.

Lindkvist Linde, *Religious Freedom and the Universal Declaration of Human Rights* (Cambridge: Cambridge University Press, 2017).

Lipset, Seymour M., *American Exceptionalism: A Double Edged Sword* (New York: W.W. Norton & Company, 1996).

Madsen, Deborah L., *American Exceptionalism* (Jackson: Mississippi University Press, 1998).

McConnell, Michael W., "Why is Religious Liberty the 'First Freedom'?," *Cardozo Law Review*, 21, (1999–2000): pp. 1243–1265.

McConnell, Michael W., "The Origins and Historical Understanding of Free Exercise of Religion," *Harvard Law Review* 103, no. 7, (1990): pp. 1409–1517.

Moyn, Samuel, "From Communist to Muslims: European Human Rights, the Cold War, and Religious Liberty," *South Atlantic Quarterly* 113, no. 1, (2014): pp. 63–86.

Noll, Mark A., "'We Shall Be as a City upon a Hill': John Winthrop's Non-American Exceptionalism", *The Review of Faith and International Affairs*, 10, no. 2, 2012, pp. 5–11.

Noonan Jr., John T., "The First Freedom and the Rehnquist Court," in Martin H. Belsky (eds.), *The Rehnquist Court. A Retrospective* (Oxford: Oxford University Press, 2002).

Onida, Francesco, "Stati Uniti d'America. Clausole religiose del primo emendamento del Bill of Rights, free exercise ed establishment della religione, controversie religiose e competenza del giudice statuale," in Francesco Margiotta Broglio, Cesare Mirabelli, Francesco Onida (eds.), *Religioni e sistemi giuridici. Introduzione al diritto ecclesiastico comparato* (Bologna: Il Mulino, 2004), pp. 255–259.

Preston, Andrew, "The First Human Right: Religious Liberty and the American Diplomatic Tradition," *The Review of Faith and International Affairs*, 11, n. 1, (2013): pp. 9–14.

Preston, Andrew, *Sword of the Spirit, Shield of Faith. Religion in American War and Diplomacy* (New York-Toronto: Knopf, 2012).

Rosenman, Samuel, *Working with Roosevelt* (New York: Harper & Brothers, 1952).

Sehat, David, *The Myth of American Religious Freedom* (New York: Oxford University Press, 2011).

Seiple, Chris, "The Essence of Exceptionalism: Roger Williams and the Birth of Religious Freedom in America," *The Review of Faith and International Affairs*, 10, no. 2, 2012, pp. 13–19.

Su, Anna L., *Exporting Freedom: Religious Liberty and American Power* (Cambridge: Harvard University Press, 2016).

Su, Anna L., "Woodrow Wilson and the Origins of the International Law of Religious Freedom," *Journal of History of International Law*, 15, (2013): pp. 235–267.

Witte jr., John and Nichols, Joel A., *Religion and the American Constitutional Experiment* (Boulder: Westview, 2010).

2 Background and genesis of the International Religious Freedom Act

1. The anticommunist initiative

Today it may seem obvious to say that Marxism-Leninism is largely defunct in the West, at least as an ideology. However, many regimes in other parts of the world still subscribe to Communist ideology, which exerts a great influence in the regulation of religious groups and the protection of religious freedom more generally.[1] The governments of China, North Korea, Vietnam, Laos, and Cuba all derive their legal systems from Marxist-Leninist principles which sharply limit religious freedom.

The inspiration and origin of the norms adopted in the United States intended to promote and protect religious freedom can be traced back to a legislative initiative designed to deal with several policies in the USSR that arose in the early 1970s that discriminated against the Jewish minority. In this period, starting in August 1972, the regime in Moscow had actually approved certain regulations intended to block people, particularly Jews, from leaving the territory of the former Soviet Union.[2] With the passage of the Jackson-Vanik amendment in 1974, the US Congress attempted to loosen the web of restrictive laws in the Soviet Union and in "non-market economy" countries in general, on the one hand offering incentives, and on the other threatening economic sanctions,[3] making respect for

1 It would be enough to think at the continuous conflicts between the Chinese Communist party and different religious groups often seen as a direct threat to the hegemony of the party.

2 For an introduction to the topic see CRS Report for Congress, *The Jackson-Vanik Amendment: A Survey*, 1/8/2005, available at: http://fas.org/sgp/crs/row/98-545.pdf.

3 For a detailed analysis of this legislation, see R.M. Dow, Linking Trade Policy to Free Emigration: The Jackson-Vanik Amendment, *Harvard Human Rights Journal*, 4, 1991, pp. 128–138. The most important amendment (2342(a)) lists all the possible measures that the government of the United States could use: "a) Actions of non-market economy countries making them ineligible for normal trade relations, program of credits, credit guarantees, or investment guarantees, or commercial agreement. To assure the continued dedication of the United States to fundamental rights, and notwithstanding any other provision of law, on or after January 3, 1975, products from non-market economy country shall not be eligible to receive non-discriminatory treatment (normal trade relations) such country shall not participate in any program of the Government of the United States which extends credits or credit guarantees or investment guarantees, directly or indirectly, and the President of the United States shall not conclude any commercial agreement with any such country, during the period beginning with the date on which the President determines such country 1) denies its citizens the right or opportunity to emigrate; 2) imposes more than a nominal tax on emigration or on the visas or other documents required for emigration, for any purposes or cause whatsoever; or 3) imposes more than a nominal tax, levy, fine, fee, or other charge on any citizen as consequence of the desire of such citizen to emigrate to the country of his choice, and ending on the date on which the President determines that such country is no longer in violation of paragraph (1), (2), (3)."

human rights – particularly the right to immigrate – a primary objective.[4] The President could then apply the economic sanctions gradually: he established the intensity of the sanctions imposed, including with regard to the states' various responses to the United States' demand for greater protection of human rights, especially the right to emigrate. The similarity between this measure and later ones in support of religious freedom is not only in the content of the legislative measures adopted (which in any case, as we will see, have significant differences), but also, and especially, the mobilization of certain political and religious groups whose contribution would become fundamental to the process of the US Congress's passing of measures in support of religious freedom.[5] According to Allen Hertzke, the measures contained in the Jackson-Vanik amendment not only helped save many Jews from the persecution of the communist Soviet regime, but later played an undoubtedly important role in the fall of that regime:

> Jackson-Vanik was hailed both as a triumph for Jewish lobbies and a foreign-policy success, which kept economic and political pressure on the Soviet Union and its client states. By shining light on how Communist systems prevented emigration, the law helped undermine the legitimacy of these regimes. When dissidents and others saw that the regime could not "pick on a few Jews" with impunity, cracks began to form in totalitarian systems that no longer looked ten feet tall.[6]

This effort on behalf of the Jews who lived in the former Soviet Union later generated the significant involvement of Jewish communities in the United States in supporting the passage of legislation protecting religious freedom, as well as initiatives supporting persecuted Christian communities throughout the world.[7] As Allen Hertzke points out, the number of Jews this law saved or helped to flee the Soviet Union remains to be empirically verified, but it is undeniable that this US initiative was imprinted onto the political and legal imagination of Jews and Christians as a weapon against the policies of persecution and repression of the brutal Communist regime.[8]

Political action by religious groups took on an essential role, not only in inspiring legislation to protect religious freedom, and specifically the Jackson-Vanik Amendment, but it

[4] This aspect is underlined in the speech made by Senator Henry Jackson made when he introduced the amendment: "We believe that there is a unique international quality about the right to free emigration [...] the right and opportunity to emigrate [...] offers a kind of ultimate relief. No matter what the cause of the cause of the desire to emigrate whether it be for the right to worship or to dissent, to publish or to speak [...] all of these and any of them can be realized by emigrating. Of freedoms, the right to emigrate is first among equals." Quoted in R.M. Dow, *Linking Trade Policy to Free Emigration: The Jackson-Vanik Amendment*, p. 129.

[5] These similarities are highlighted by Allen Hertzke: "[...] campaign tactics on behalf of persecuted religious minorities mirror those employed by Jews nearly three decade previous. Fostering public awareness through dramatic media exposure, personalizing the persecution, mobilizing congregations, and mounting constituency pressure – thus making the issue one that members of Congress and executive branch officials could not ignore." See Allen D. Hertzke, *Freeing God's Children. The Unlikely Alliance for Global Human Rights* (Lanham: Rowan & Littlefield, 2004), p. 75.

[6] *Ibid.*, p. 76.

[7] Many of them were members of the cultural and political élite of the United States: "Preeminent, of course, was Michael Hoowitz, who made the problem his personal crusade. But Horowitz was joined by a broad cross section of Jewish leadership." *Ibid.*, pp. 77–78.

[8] *Ibid.*, p. 133.

also had fundamental importance in the process which, in later years, and especially after the fall of the Berlin Wall, led to the 1998 approval of the International Religious Freedom Act. The significance of the political transition of the former Communist countries is also noted by Allen Hertzke, who points out that the election of Karol Wojtyla as Pontifex of the Catholic Church in 1978, and his privileged relationship with the United States on the matter of religious freedom, influenced developments in this area.[9]

Thus, the more recent interest in the promotion of religious freedom has deep roots in the Cold War. It is the result of a boiling magma of events and interests coagulated around this notion of the "Persecuted Church," which animates numerous anti-Communist sentiments in the various Christian communities in Communist countries who are subject to oppression and restrictions on their freedom. It is also the fruit of the growing post-WWII interest in the promotion and protection of international human rights,[10] and the result of a historical process in which US policies have always been particularly attentive to the internationalization of policies for the protection and promotion of religious freedom.[11]

2. The role of religious organizations

Thus the end of Communism favored the activism of religious organizations and movements that sought out new spaces in contexts where they had always been met with hostility. Persecution against Christian minorities in the world was certainly one of the primary factors in the formation of a joint coalition of lay and religious organizations, which would be decisive in placing religious freedom at the center of US foreign policy. Added to this, on the domestic front, was the Supreme Court ruling in the *Smith* case, which further contributed to the mobilization of religious organizations and other groups seeking greater protection of religious freedom. On the one hand, there was the influence of a huge group of different Christian organizations – including Voice of the Martyrs, Open Doors, International Christian Concern, Persecution Project Foundation, Christian Freedom International, and Compass Direct; on the other there was the primary role played by Washington political elites, especially certain members of Congress who were particularly sympathetic to the appeals of religious groups. In 1996 one of these, Christopher Smith, organized the first hearing of the United States Congress on the subject of the persecution of Christians and

9 As Allen Hertzke highlights: "As an Eastern European cleric, Wojtyla experienced Nazi and Communist attempts to eradicate the Church as an independent force, and he helped lead the Church in resistance for a quarter century." Karol Wojtyla, on July 23, 2001, expressed his personal gratitude to George W. Bush for the US policy of promotion of religious freedom: "It is significant that the promotion of religious freedom continues to be an important goal of American foreign policy in the International community. I gladly express the appreciation of the whole Catholic Church for America's commitment in this regard." *Ibid.*, pp. 117, 119.

10 On the two issues see Elizabeth A. Castelli, "Praying for the Persecuted Church: US Christian Activism in the Global Arena," *Journal of Human Rights* 4, (2005): pp. 321–351. As I have highlighted before it was also the "myth" of American religious freedom that influenced the interest in the issue: "The emergent mandate for political action and international solidarity in the US movement is grounded in a range of familiar discourses: ideals of 'Americanness' and American exceptionalism, themselves grounded in (a somewhat rosy version of) American history; traditional liberal ideals of tolerance and freedom; and the language and authority of international (and, importantly for these advocates, universal) human rights." *Ibid.*, p. 322.

11 See Anna L. Su, *Exporting Freedom: Religious Liberty and American Power.*

Jews.[12] In that same year, then-Secretary of State Warren Christopher created an Advisory Committee on Religious Freedom Abroad[13] inside the State Department. The Committee's mission was to come up with ways to integrate the right of religious freedom into the Department's policies. As Gregorio Bettiza[14] has noted, the issue of religious persecution began to appear in 1999, including in documents on National Security Strategy,[15] which some years later would refer to religious freedom as a true priority.[16]

Although it is true that the initiative for the passage of specific legislative measures to promote and protect religious freedom was broadly shared, we cannot fail to note that religious movements closely connected to conservative evangelicals played a primary role, promoting appeals by those who saw the persecution of Christians throughout the world as an opportunity for practical action in the United States.[17] As Lee Marsden states:

> The increasing focus on religious persecution and a commitment to taking religious freedom as seriously as other aspects of freedom and democracy by the US government was largely achieved by pressure from the Christian Right. The International Religious

12 U.S. Congress, *Persecution of Christians Worldwide: Hearing Before the Subcommittee on International Operations and Human Rights of the Committee on International Relation, House of Representatives*, One Hundred Fourth Congress, Second Session, 15/2/1996.

13 This was a very important step in the framework of the construction of the International Religious Freedom Act and religious groups played an important role: "The Committee was influenced by the many faith-based organizations that began lobbying the U.S. Congress to pay greater attention to human rights during the 1980's and 1990's. The Committee consisting of 20 American religious leaders and scholars, produced an interim report in 1998 and a final draft in 1999 that recommended a foreign policy agenda geared toward the promotion of religious freedom worldwide. At the same time, the U.S. Congress, faith-based nongovernmental organizations, and the Department of State began discussing ways to integrate religious freedom initiatives into U.S. foreign policy. The product of these debates was the *International Religious Freedom Act of 1998*." See Department of State-Bureau of Democracy, Human Rights and Labour, "History of the Office of International Religious Freedom," 2001, available at: http://2001–2009.state.gov/g/drl/irf/fs/2298.htm. The Committee had a very specific mandate that was specified at the time of its creation: "[…] call attention to problems of religious persecution and other violations of religious freedom, and religious intolerance abroad and advise on how to end them; and to provide information on how to bring about reconciliation in areas of conflict, especially conflicts where religion is a factor, and promote respect for human rights so that religious freedom can be fully enjoyed." See Advisory Committee on Religious Freedom Abroad, "Interim Report to the Secretary of State and to the President of the United States," 23/1/1998, available at: https://1997–2001.state.gov/www/global/human_rights/980123_acrfa_interim.html.

14 Gregorio Bettiza, *The Global Resurgence of Religion and the Desecularization of American Foreign Policy*, 1990–2012, Ph.D. dissertation defended at the London School of Economics in August 2012.

15 For instance, according to a 1997 report: "A disturbing aspect of the post-Cold War world has been the persistence, and in some cases the intensification, of religious intolerance, religious persecution, and the exploitation of religious and ethnic differences for narrow and violent ends. In 1996 many religious groups around the world continued to face persecution and other difficulties in practicing their faiths and maintaining their cultural loyalties." Quoted *ibid.*, p. 169.

16 This happened with the National Security Strategy of 1999: "The promotion of religious freedom is one of the highest concerns in our foreign policy. Freedom of thought, conscience and religion is a bedrock issue for the American people." Quoted *ibid.*

17 There were several people and non-governmental organizations involved. As Mohd Afandi Salleh underlines: "[…] the coalition was arguably one of the most important efforts of evangelicals that contributed to the introduction of the IRFA. Their ability to establish contacts and alliances with other conservative movements or organizations such as the neo-conservatives, Jews, Catholics, Muslims and other religions made the international religious freedom issue become a hot topic at US official level"; Salleh lists some of the most important people that took part in this movement: "They were Charles Colson

Freedom Act and the mandate to record progress on religious freedom throughout the world are notable advances that would not have been achieved without them.[18]

Jeremy Gunn points out, however, that the regulations subsequently approved reflect not only these appeals, but are the result of a much more complex political arrangement.[19] The role of religious conservatives can be attributed to the dynamics of domestic US policy on the one hand, and on the other, the already-widespread perception of discrimination and persecution against Christians on a global level, particularly in Muslim countries and those still under the control of Communist regimes. In this regard, Nina Shea's[20] fundamental contribution, *In the Lion's Den*,[21] highlights the persecution against Christian communities in those countries.[22]

Michael Horowitz's political and media campaign, initiated in 1995, was fundamental to the approval of the International Religious Freedom Act. This initiative started with the publication of what would become a famous *Wall Street Journal* editorial,[23] and with the

of the Prison Fellowship, Richard Land of the Southern Baptist Convention, Gary Bauer of the Family Research Council, James Dobson of Focus on the Family, Daniel Hodel and Ralph Reed of the Christian Coalition and many others." See Mohd A. Salleh, "The International Religious Freedom Act of 1998 and the Role of Religious Movements," *Malaysian Journal of History, Politics and Strategic Studies* 38, no. 2, (2011): p. 29. See also Bryan J. Hehir, "Religious Freedom and U.S. Foreign Policy: Categories and Choices," in Elliot Abrams (eds.), *The Influence of Faith: Religious Groups and U.S. Foreign Policy* (Lanham: Rowan & Littlefield, 2001), p. 49 and Nina Shea, "The Origins and Legacy of the Movement to Fight Religious Persecution," *The Review of Faith and International Affairs* 6, no. 2, (2008): pp. 25–26.

18 Lee Mardsen, *For God's Sake: The Christian Right and U.S. Foreign Policy* (London: Zed Books, 2008), p. 146.

19 Jeremy Gunn, "American Exceptionalism and Globalist Double Standard: A More Balanced Alternative," *Columbia Journal of Transnational Law* 41, (2002–2003): pp. 137–152.

20 Nina Shea was deeply influenced in her choice to devote her efforts to fight religious persecutions by a visit to Nicaragua at that time governed by the principles of Marxism-Leninism. See Allen D. Hertzke, *Freeing God's Children. The Unlikely Alliance for Global Human Rights*, p. 121.

21 See Nina Shea, *In the Lion's Den. A Shocking Account of Persecution and Martyrdom of Christians Today and How We Should Respond* (Nashville: Broadman & Holman, 1997). Already from the introduction the author underlines how militant Islamism and communism were the two constant threats for the freedom of Christians: "Around the globe, these two ideologies have consistently oppressed Christians, as well as other independent groups and individuals. While there are cases of persecution of Christian minorities by Hindus, Buddhists, and even by other dominant Christian groups, it is anti-Christian persecution by communism and militant Islam that, because of their global sweep and virulence, poses the great threat." *Ibid.*, p. 1.

22 In 1996 Nina Shea organized an important conference with Michael Horowitz. According to Mohd Afandi Salleh the conference was of fundamental importance in raising awareness of the topic of religious persecutions: "Shea played a crucial role and became a testifying to the issue of religious persecution around the world. Finally, at the summit, the National Association of Evangelicals released a 'Statement of Conscience' that declared the would 'do what is within our power to the end that the Government of the United States will take appropriate action to combat the intolerable religious persecution now victimizing fellow believers and those of other faiths." See Mohd A. Salleh, *The International Religious Freedom Act of 1998 and the Role of Religious Movement*, p. 32.

23 Michael Horowitz, "New Intolerance between Crescent and Cross," *The Wall Street Journal*, 5/7/1995. For Allen Hertzke the role of Michael Horowitz, also as a Jew, was of fundamental importance in order to avoid the association between the initiative and the religious right: "Enlisting Jewish support for the antipersecution movement was crucial, because it helped inoculate a movement that could have been caricatured as a Christian Right front." See Allen D. Hertzke, *Freeing God's Children. The Unlikely Alliance for Global Human Rights*, p. 153.

subsequent drafting of the Statement of Conscience,[24] approved by the National Association of Evangelicals. Central to the vision of Michael Horowitz and conservative leaders, particularly evangelicals, was the criticism of the secularization and marginalization of religion in public life. The protection of religious minorities – particularly Christians – in other parts of the world became a sign of hope for reversing the damage done by a social phenomenon they considered deplorable.

Equally significant was the political battle waged against the violations of religious freedom committed by the regime in Sudan, where Christians were subject to persecution.[25] The mobilization of US Christian religious groups was vitally important in this case as well.[26] In 1983, in the wake of the Iranian revolution, the ever-present rivalries in Sudan intensified when fundamentalist Islamic militants took power.[27] From this point on, the extermination of Christian minorities became one of the objectives of the regime, which committed a true genocide.[28] The process that led to the 1998 approval of the International Religious Freedom Act was therefore the result of a long political process whose beginnings can be traced to the mid-90s but whose roots, as we have seen, are much older.

3. The initial projects of the Clinton administration and the International Religious Freedom Act

In 1996, the movement against the persecution of Christians finally succeeded in bringing the subject of violation of religious freedom to the attention of the Clinton administration. In fact, in that year, for the first time, the International Operations and Human Rights Subcommittee of the House of Representatives organized a hearing on the persecution of Christians and Jews throughout the world.[29] At first, Michael Horowitz was inspired by the model of the Jackson-Vanik Act, and although it could have been useful to attempt to pass a law on the persecution of Christian minorities, some members of Congress said that there should be a general reference to religious freedom, understood as a right to be defended and promoted for all individuals. It was only in May 1997 that Frank Wolf, a member of the House of Representatives, introduced the bill entitled "The Freedom From Religious Persecution Act," which created an office to monitor religious persecution and impose sanctions on countries responsible for the persecution of religious minorities. The

24 See National Association of Evangelicals, *Statement of Conscience Concerning Worldwide Religious Persecution*, 1996, available at: http://goo.gl/H5KM4J.

25 On the centrality of this event in the context of the wider debate on protection and promotion of religious freedom by the United States of America see Melani McAllister, "U.S. Evangelicals and the Politics of Slave Redemption as Religious Freedom in Sudan," *The South Atlantic Quarterly* 113, no. 1, (2014): pp. 87–108.

26 In this case the alliance against the regime in Khartoum brings together liberals and conservatives: "The Sudan alliance spans the cultural divide, with the liberal leaders of Reform Judaism working side by side with representatives of the Southern Baptist Convention." See Allen D. Hertzke, *Freeing God's Children. The Unlikely Alliance for Global Human Rights*, p. 239.

27 At the end of the 1980s Sudan offered refuge and hospitality to Osama Bin Laden.

28 According to Allen Hertzke, besides the ethnic conflict, the most important one was the religious one: "Though the regime targets animists and Muslim who resist its fundamentalism, it has literally attempted to wipe out Christianity, which historically provided the cultural glue for the south." See Allen D. Hertzke, *Freeing God's Children. The Unlikely Alliance for Global Human Rights*, p. 243.

29 U.S. Congress, Persecution of Christians Worldwide: *Hearing Before the Subcommittee on International Operations and Human Rights of the Committee on International Relations, House of Representatives.*

bill foresaw the creation of a Director of Religious Persecution Monitoring,[30] responsible for designating a specific religious community as being persecuted in a country, in order to facilitate asylum requests for religious persecution. However, it made no provisions for the creation of a specific Commission on the model that would later be instituted, or the drafting of an annual report. The term "persecution" was included in the title of the bill. Its purpose was to focus attention on the most severe cases of violation of religious freedom, defined as "widespread and ongoing persecution,"[31] to produce a general effect of protection of that right.

A fundamental characteristic of the Wolf proposal was a system of automatic sanctions for violations of religious freedom, eliminating political discretion in their application. This idea was representative of the spirit in which Frank Wolf interpreted the problem of persecution of Christian minorities: a battle of good against evil, in support of which the United States must use all its economic, political, and diplomatic power.[32] The Clinton administration, however, immediately opposed the automatic sanctions.[33] First, it was difficult to arrive at a precise legal definition of "religious persecution," and this caused some members of Congress to fear that the regulations set out by the bill could be manipulated or exploited. Furthermore, such sanctions could have been completely inapplicable, given the extremely detailed definition that ended up in the text proposed by Wolf and Specter.[34] Some State Department diplomats raised some issues around the uncertain location of the office for monitoring religious persecution, and the over-broad discretion of the office's director in applying sanctions.[35] It should be clarified, however, that the bill provided that sanctions

30 As Laura Bryant Handford underlines, this unit: "[...] made finding regarding any entity or country he or she deemed guilty of egregious religious persecution, defined to include such acts as crucifixion, widespread killings, etc." See Laura B. Handford, "The International Religious Freedom Act: Sources, Policy, Influence," *The Review of Faith and International Affairs* 6, no. 2, (2008): p. 34.

31 As Allen Hertzke reminds us: "[...] the bill focused on 'widespread and ongoing persecution of persons on account of their personal beliefs', including abduction, enslavement, killing, imprisonment, forced resettlement, rape or crucifixion or other forms of torture." See Allen D. Hertzke, *Freeing God's Children. The Unlikely Alliance for Global Human Rights*, p. 191.

32 For Allen Hertzke this is the result of the personality and way to understand political conflict of Frank Wolf: "In Frank Wolf, Horowitz found a kindred spirit, a fervent moralist who sees justice in stark terms. As one staffer put it, Wolf is 'not a cautious person', but a visionary." *Ibid.*, p. 188.

33 This was one of the key critical aspects of the proposal: "In sum, FFRPA was both too blunt an instrument and too narrow in scope – likely never to be implemented because of its automatic, uncalibrated sanctions, yet paradoxically holding the potential to wreak havoc if its measures were imposed with no regard to context, likelihood of success, or potential backlash." See Laura B. Handford, *The International Religious Freedom Act: Sources, Policy, Influence*, p. 35.

34 This aspect is highlighted by William Imboden that took part to the drafting process of the International Religious Freedom Act: "Wolf-Specter uses very explicitly, from its title, definitions, and language throughout the bill, the term 'religious persecution'. And it defines 'religious persecution' to include only the most severe and violent acts against people for their religious faith that occur, as the original draft of the bill said, 'in a widespread, systematic and ongoing fashion'. Perhaps only one or two rogue nations might be guilty under this definition, so Wolf-Specter had a very narrow purview." See William Imboden, transcription of an oral intervention in Rosalind I.J. Hackett and Mark Silk, David Hoover (eds.), *Religious Persecution as a U.S. Policy Issue*, Proceedings of a Consultation held at Trinity College, Hartford, 26–27/9/1999, p. 12, available at: http://goo.gl/8JPtsM.

35 This is, for instance, the analysis offered by Thomas Farr: "The centerpiece of the Wolf-Specter bill was the director of the office of religious persecution monitoring. In the original bill and its immediate successor (introduced in May and September 1997, respectively), the director was to be appointed by the President and the monitoring office placed in the President's executive office, rather than at the

ultimately be made at the sole discretion of the President of the United States, who would have had to provide adequate justification to the Congress for the decision.

Several senators, including Republican Don Nickles, feared repercussions against Christian missionaries, and so were against the automatic sanctions systems set out in the Wolf bill. According to Nickles, this system did not provide the necessary flexibility to manage the various contexts and scenarios in which violations of religious freedom occurred; an appropriate contextualization was necessary to ensure the correct approach and appropriate solutions.[36] As one of the drafters of the next bill, William Inboden, pointed out: "It almost could be characterized as a 'do-nothing' bill. If you have only the option, metaphorically speaking, of using a nuclear scale weapon against a country or doing nothing, a lot of times you will do nothing." Thus Don Nickles presented his own bill called the "International Religious Freedom Act."[37] But this attempt fared no better, as it was held hostage to repeated vetoes.[38] A final text was approved only in October 1998, combining the work of the sponsors of the two previous bills.

State Department. The director would have extraordinary powers to punish but very little influence (or required interest in) addressing the underlying structures of persecution, let alone advancing religious freedom." See Thomas F. Farr, *World of Faith and Freedom. Why International Religious Liberty is Vital to American National Security* (New York: Oxford University Press, 2008), p. 117.

36 This contradiction is once again underlined by William Imboden: "To put it simply, Wolf-Specter would have treated countries like China, Egypt, Pakistan, Israel, Saudi Arabia, Iran and North Korea all the same. And as you know, some of these countries are allies of the United States, and others are almost our mortal enemies. With some we have strong economic ties, while with others we don't have any economic relationship. Some persecute just Christians; others persecute people of many different faiths. It seemed to us perhaps not as responsible or as effective an approach to use the same measures in response to 'persecution' when so many different variables exist." See William Inboden, transcription of an oral intervention in Rosalind I.J. Hackett, Mark Silk and David Hoover (ed.), *Religious Persecution as a U.S. Policy Issue*, Proceedings of a Consultation held at Trinity College, pp. 12–13.

37 *Ibid.*, p. 13.

38 According to Steven Wales the fact that the text was not approved was also the result of technical and political variables: "Opponents of both religious persecution bills included USA Engage – a coalition of exporters who paid for lobbying against the two bills, the National Foreign Trade Council, and the National Council of Churches. In addition 'free trade Republicans' Senator Rod Grams of Minnesota and Chuck Hagel of Nebraska blocked a vote on the Nickles bill." Besides these lobbying actions there were also divisions within the Republican Party: "'Social conservatives' wanted to protect global religious freedom while 'economic conservatives' sought to protect global free trade." See Steven Wales, "Remembering the Persecuted. An Analysis of the International Religious Freedom Act," *Houston Journal of International Law* 24, no. 3, (2002): pp. 587, 588.

References

Advisory Committee on Religious Freedom Abroad, "Interim Report to the Secretary of State and to the President of the United States," 23/1/1998, available at: https://1997-2001.state.gov/www/global/human_rights/980123_acrfa_interim.html.

Bettiza, Gregorio, *The Global Resurgence of Religion and the Desecularization of American Foreign Policy*, 1990–2012, Ph.D. dissertation defended at the London School of Economics in August 2012.

Bryan J., Hehir, "Religious Freedom and U.S. Foreign Policy: Categories and Choices," in Elliot Abrams (eds.), *The Influence of Faith: Religious Groups and U.S. Foreign Policy* (Lanham: Rowan & Littlefield, 2001), pp. 33–54.

Castelli, Elizabeth A., "Praying for the Persecuted Church: US Christian Activism in the Global Arena," *Journal of Human Rights* 4, (2005): pp. 321–351.

CRS Report for Congress, *The Jackson-Vanik Amendment: A Survey*, 1/8/2005, available at: http://fas.org/sgp/crs/row/98–545.pdf

Department of State-Bureau of Democracy, Human Rights and Labour, "History of the Office of International Religious Freedom," 2001, available at: http://2001–2009.state.gov/g/drl/irf/fs/2298.htm.

Dow, R.M., Linking Trade Policy to Free Emigration: The Jackson-Vanik Amendment, *Harvard Human Rights Journal*, 4, 1991, pp. 128–138.

Farr, Thomas F., *World of Faith and Freedom. Why International Religious Liberty is Vital to American National Security* (New York: Oxford University Press, 2008).

Gunn, Jeremy, "American Exceptionalism and Globalist Double Standard: A More Balanced Alternative," *Columbia Journal of Transnational Law* 41, (2002–2003): pp. 137–152.

Handford, Laura B., "The International Religious Freedom Act: Sources, Policy, Influence," *The Review of Faith and International Affairs* 6, no. 2, (2008): pp. 33–39.

Hertzke, Allen D., *Freeing God's Children. The Unlikely Alliance for Global Human Rights* (Lanham: Rowan & Littlefield, 2004).

Horowitz, Michael, "New Intolerance between Crescent and Cross," *The Wall Street Journal*, 5/7/1995.

Imboden, William, transcription of an oral intervention in Rosalind I.J. Hackett, Mark Silk, and David Hoover (eds.), *Religious Persecution as a U.S. Policy Issue*, Proceedings of a Consultation held at Trinity College, Hartford, 26–27/9/1999.

Mardsen, Lee, *For God's Sake: The Christian Right and U.S. Foreign Policy* (London: Zed Books, 2008).

McAllister, Melani, "U.S. Evangelicals and the Politics of Slave Redemption as Religious Freedom in Sudan," *The South Atlantic Quarterly* 113, no. 1, (2014): pp. 87–108.

National Association of Evangelicals, *Statement of Conscience Concerning Worldwide Religious Persecution*, 1996, available at: http://goo.gl/H5KM4J.

Salleh, Mohd A., "The International Religious Freedom Act of 1998 and the Role of Religious Movements," *Malaysian Journal of History, Politics and Strategic Studies* 38, no. 2, (2011): pp. 27–44.

Shea, Nina, "The Origins and Legacy of the Movement to Fight Religious Persecution," *The Review of Faith and International Affairs* 6, no. 2, (2008): pp. 25–31.

Shea, Nina, *In the Lion's Den. A Shocking Account of Persecution and Martyrdom of Christians Today and How We Should Respond* (Nashville: Broadman & Holman, 1997).

Su, Anna L., *Exporting Freedom: Religious Liberty and American Power* (Cambridge: Harvard University Press, 2016).

U.S. Congress, *Persecution of Christians Worldwide: Hearing Before the Subcommittee on International Operations and Human Rights of the Committee on International Relation, House of Representatives*, One Hundred Fourth Congress, Second Session, 15/2/1996.

Wales, Steven, "Remembering the Persecuted. An Analysis of the International Religious Freedom Act," *Houston Journal of International Law* 24, no. 3, (2002): pp. 579–648.

3 The International Religious Freedom Act

1. The role of the Department of State and the United States Commission on International Religious Freedom

Understanding the origins and objectives that led to the approval of the International Religious Freedom Act, and studying its regulatory and institutional architecture, is fundamental to understanding even a few of the later initiatives that the United States undertook in the area of protection of human rights.[1] Indeed, with the approval of the International Religious Freedom Act, the promotion and protection of religious freedom became an integral part of US foreign policy. If religious freedom up to this point had been a foundational myth and part of the history of the United States, thenceforth it would become an important tool in relations with other states. This aspect can clearly be seen in the words of President Bill Clinton on the day of the bill's passage in Congress:

> The United States was founded on the right to worship freely and on respect for the right of others to worship as they believe. My Administration has made religious freedom a central element of U.S. foreign policy. When we promote religious freedom we also promote freedom of expression, conscience, and association, and other human rights. This Act is not directed against any one country or religious faith. Indeed, this Act will serve to promote the religious freedom of people of all backgrounds, whether Muslim, Christian, Jewish, Buddhist, Hindu, Taoist or any other faith.[2]

These are the four main points that form the basis for US action. First, as we have already seen, for the first time in history the protection and promotion of religious freedom became an integral part of US foreign policy; second, the United States agreed to provide assistance to newly democratic countries to carry out the protection of religious freedom; third, measures were set out in support of nongovernmental organizations and religious groups; and finally, it set out a specific system of sanctioning measures for countries that violate religious

[1] This aspect is underlined by Allen Hertzke: "In the ecology of human rights, the struggle for the IRFA shaped the environment for future initiatives. Without IRFA there would be no *Sudan Peace Act*; without the religious advocacy coalition, there would be no human rights trafficking law. The religious freedom campaign represents a kind of liminal moment in the politics of human rights." See Allen D. Hertzke, *Freeing God's Children. The Unlikely Alliance for Global Human Rights*, p. 184.

[2] William J. Clinton, *Statement on Signing the International Religious Freedom Act of 1998*, 27/10/1998, available at: http://goo.gl/8V6LF2

freedom.[3] In addition to President Clinton's speech, the exceptional quality of the history of religious freedom in the United States is also invoked in the preamble to the International Religious Freedom Act.[4] The preamble frames religious freedom in the broader context of agreements under international law, taking into account reports documenting numerous instances of discrimination and persecution against the faithful of various religious communities.[5] The second section (b) identifies the policies that the United States must follow. These are divided into five categories: 1) the condemnation of violations of religious freedom and the promotion of religious freedom; 2) based on the Foreign Assistance Act of 1961 and the International Financial Institution Act of 1977, the commitment to allocate funds to assist countries that are not gross violators of religious freedom; 3) applying the measures set out by regulations that are "vigorous and flexible," also taking into account US relations with various countries; 4) the need for a multilateral and cooperative approach with other countries; 5) making use of all possible instruments available to US diplomacy for the promotion of religious freedom.

Title I concerns the activity of the State Department and the appointment of the Ambassador at Large for International Religious Freedom. The appointment of the Ambassador is entrusted to the President of the United States, who must make his or her decision through the "advice and consent" procedure of the Senate. The Ambassador at Large must first take every action necessary for the promotion of religious freedom; for this purpose, he or she may denounce violations and suggest the appropriate response by the US government.[6] The Ambassador also has a consulting role as principal advisor to the President on matters pertaining to religious freedom, in cooperation with the US Commission on International Religious Freedom,[7] and a diplomatic role in problems that concern religious freedom.[8]

Section 102 of the International Religious Freedom Act introduces the responsibility for monitoring religious freedom in the world, with the additional requirements of producing an

[3] Mohd A. Salleh, *The International Religious Freedom Act of 1998 and the Role of Religious Movement*, pp. 32–33.

[4] A clear example is given by section two: "The right to freedom of religion undergirds the very origin and existence of the United States. Many of our Nation's founders fled religious persecution abroad, cherishing in their hearts and minds the ideal of religious freedom. They established in law, as a fundamental right and as a pillar of our Nation, the right to freedom of religion. From its birth to this day, the United States has prized this legacy of religious freedom and honored this heritage by standing for religious freedom and offering refuge to those suffering religious persecution." See U.S. Congress, *International Religious Freedom Act of 1998*, sec. 2.

[5] *Ibid.*, sec 2 (4): "More than one-half of the world's population lives under regimes that severely restrict or prohibit the freedom of their citizens to study, believe, observe, and freely practice the religious faith of their choice. Religious believers and communities suffer both government-sponsored and government-tolerated violations of their rights to religious freedom."

[6] *Ibid.*, title I (c). Until today have served in this position: Robert Seiple (May 1999–September 2000), John Handford (May 2002–January 2009), Suzan Johnson Cook (May 2011–July 2014), David Saperstein (December 2014–January 2017).

[7] The advisory activity is focused on two specific issues: "A) the policy of the United States Government toward governments that violate freedom of religion or that fail to ensure the individual's right to religious belief and practice; B) policies that advance the right to religious freedom abroad."

[8] See U.S. Congress, *International Religious Freedom Act of 1998*, sec. 101 (b) (3) (A): [...] contacts with foreign governments, intergovernmental organizations, and specialized agencies of the United Nations, the Organization on Security and Cooperation in Europe, and other international organizations of which the United States is a member; B) multilateral conferences and meetings relevant to religious freedom abroad."

annual report, drafted in cooperation with the State Department, which must then be sent to Congress. It also sets out a detailed description of the actions taken by the United States for the promotion of religious freedom abroad and the international conventions in force. A specific section is also dedicated to the training of diplomats on the topic of religious freedom.[9]

Title II of the International Religious Freedom Act establishes the US Commission on International Religious Freedom and sets out its rules. In addition to the Ambassador at Large, who participates in its activities as a non-voting member, the commission is made up of nine commissioners. Three are directly appointed by the President, another three by the President of the Senate, and the final three by the President of the House of Representatives. With regard to the last two appointments, a system of weighting between minority and majority is set out to ensure fair representation inside the Commission. Commissioners must possess sufficient experience in the field of human rights and religious freedom. The appointment is for two years and may be renewed only once. Section 202 defines the responsibilities of the Commission, categorizing them along two main lines: monitoring and reporting on situations of violation of religious freedom, and consulting with the President, Secretary of State, and Congress on matters of religious freedom.[10] The activities of the Commission are then set out in the annual report, to be submitted, under Section 203, no later than May 1 of each year to the President, Secretary of State, and Congress. The commissioners have the right to express dissenting opinions on the results of the Commission's monitoring and related recommendations.[11]

Up to this point, the Commission has acted as a true watchdog[12] for religious freedom, and in some cases its evaluations have diverged, sometimes considerably, from those given in the State Department's annual report. An emblematic example of this is the recent designation of Saudi Arabia as a "country of particular concern," as Saudi Arabia is often ignored by the State Department for reasons of *realpolitik*, given the alliance that exists in many dossiers with regard to foreign policy between the United States and the Saudi monarchy.[13]

9 According to section 708 this training should include: "1) instruction on International documents and United States policy in human rights, which shall be mandatory for all members of the Service having reporting responsibilities relating to human rights and for chief of missions; 2) instruction on the internationally recognized right to freedom of religion, the nature, activities and beliefs of different religions, and the various aspects and manifestations of violations of religious freedom." *Ibid.*, sec. 708.

10 It is also possible to distinguish between "Policy review and recommendations in response to violations" and "Policy review and recommendations in response to progress." However it remains central the monitoring activity defined in section 202 (e): "The Commission shall, on an ongoing basis, monitor facts and circumstances of violations of religious freedom, in consultation with independent human rights groups and non-governmental organizations, including churches and other religious communities, and make such recommendations as may be necessary to the appropriate officials and offices in the United States Government." *Ibid.* sec 202 (e).

11 *Ibid.*, sec. 205 (c).

12 This is the definition used by Allen Hertzke: "[...] a watchdog and policy advocate, the commission provides an independent assessment of the status of religious freedom, critiques the State Department report, and offers detailed policy recommendations." See Allen D. Hertzke, *Freeing God's Children. The Unlikely Alliance for Global Human Rights*, p. 305.

13 As Allen Hertzke reminds us in case of designation there would have been the possibility of sanctions as provided by the International Religious Freedom Act and this would have been a problem being Saudia Arabia an allied country. Also Robert Seipel, first Ambassador for religious freedom, underlined this problem: "Playing its watchdog role, the commission took Seiple to task for these statements, calling them 'inexplicable' given that State Department's own report admits that 'freedom of religion does not exist' in the Kingdom." Quoted in Allen D. Hertzke, *ibid.*, p. 308.

Despite the substantial differences in some of the evaluations made by the two institutions, we can say in any case that this tension is one of the structural aspects of the system set out by the International Religious Freedom Act. Many of the promoters of this legislation feared that short-term political calculations by the State Department could lead to the inaccurate representation of persecution in the annual reports, and therefore an insufficient defense of religious freedom. It was precisely for this reason that the US Commission on International Religious Freedom, less bound up with the motivations of the State Department and US foreign policy, was able to act with greater religious freedom and denounce violations of religious freedom with greater force.[14]

Therefore, as Allen Hertzke has stated, even when analyses of data and information vary, the two institutions work synergistically: "While the commission feels free to criticize U.S. diplomacy, it actually works closely with the State Department, and commissioners argue that if there is tension at times, it is healthy."[15]

2. The role and actions of the President of the United States

Title IV of the International Religious Freedom Act defines the actions available to the President of the United States to fight violations of religious freedom. First, Section 401 sets out a distinction between responding to violations of religious freedom and promoting religious freedom, which does not require the existence of violations and is set out as an objective of US foreign policy. The President's decisions and actions are based on the information contained in the country reports prepared by the diplomatic network of the State Department and an annual report drafted by the US Commission on International Religious Freedom and its recommendations. The President's decisions on the measures to be adopted must, however, be guided by the principle of proportionality, and must have the final goal of concluding an agreement with the country accused of violating religious freedom in order to end the violation as soon as possible.[16] Section 402 sets out and governs the actions to be taken: those of particular importance include the annual designation of countries named as being "of particular concern for religious freedom." This designation is intended to indicate countries where violations of religious freedom are particularly severe.[17] It must be made based on the information available, and in particular, the decision to make the designation is based on the reports and instructions of the US Commission on International Religious Freedom. In the designation, the President must indicate which foreign government bodies are to be held responsible for the violations and, once the designation is made, notify the relevant Congressional committee.

[14] This analysis is offered by Thomas Farr. According to him: "The role of the commission was initially envisioned to be that of a 'truth patrol', established for a limited time to ensure that the State Department did not fudge the facts. It reflected the concern of many across the political spectrum that the real story of religious persecution was not being told, either by the mainstream press or by the State Department's annual Human Rights Report." See Thomas F. Farr, *World of Faith and Freedom. Why International Religious Liberty is Vital to American National Security*, p. 119.

[15] Allen D. Hertzke, *Freeing God's Children. The Unlikely Alliance for Global Human Rights*, p. 309.

[16] See U.S. Congress, *International Religious Freedom Act of 1998*, sec. 401 (c): "[...] when appropriate, make every reasonable effort to conclude a binding agreement concerning the cessation of such violations in countries with which the United States has diplomatic relations."

[17] *Ibid.*, sec. 402 (b).

Section 405 of the International Religious Freedom Act describes the fifteen instruments that the President of the United States may make use of in the protection and promotion of religious freedom. These include the classic diplomatic instruments such as public condemnation and the cancellation of cultural exchanges and visits to violating countries. Economic sanctions play a particularly important role, especially those concerning the cancellation of development aid.[18] However, the goal of stopping the violation takes top priority, including through a binding agreement with the foreign government.[19] The International Religious Freedom Act also sets out, under certain conditions, the possibility of exemptions from sanctions.[20] In any case, the sanctions last for two years, after which they may be renewed by the President.[21] It also sets out the exclusion of the decisions of judicial powers over presidential determinations.[22]

3. The promotion of religious freedom

What space does the International Religious Freedom Act grant to the true promotion of religious freedom? Supporters of the law maintain that the measure supports a true Copernican revolution that makes the protection of religious freedom a fundamental priority of US foreign policy. Skeptics such as Thomas Farr note instead that, going beyond the enthusiastic rhetoric, the text of the law and the measures adopted have not had a substantial effect. According to Farr, this is also true for the bills submitted prior to approval of the International Religious Freedom Act. He writes:

> Ironically, neither Wolf-Specter nor (despite its title) the International Religious Freedom Act had as a major goal the promotion of religious freedom. Both focused primarily on identifying and reacting to the activities of persecuting governments. The IRF Act paid rhetorical homage to religious freedom but devoted only a brief

18 According to point 9 of the section: "The withdrawal, limitation, or suspension of the United States development assistance in accordance with section 116 of the Foreign Assistance Act of 1961," and: "Directing and Export-Import Bank of the United States, the Overseas Private Investment Corporation, or the Trade and Development Agency not to approve the issuance of any (or specified number of) guarantees, insurance, extension of credit, or participations in the extension of credit with respect to specific government, agency, instrumentality, or official found, or determined by the President to be responsible for violations under sections 401 or 402." It is also worth, among the others, pointing at the measures foreseen by points (14) and (15): "Prohibiting any United States financial institution from making loans or providing credits totaling more than $ 10,000,000 in any 12 month period to the specific foreign government, agency, instrumentality, or official found or determined by the President to be responsible for violations under section 401 or 402" and also: "Prohibiting the United States Government from procuring or entering into any contract for the procurement of, any goods or services from the foreign government, entities, or official found or determined by the President to be responsible for violations under section 401 or 402," *ibid.*

19 According to sec. 405, 15 (c): "The entry into force of a binding agreement for the cessation of the violations shall be a primary objective for the President in responding to a foreign government that has engaged in or tolerated particularly severe violations of religious freedom." It is however impossible to impose sanctions that restrict the supply of medicines or any other kind of humanitarian assistance, *ibid.*, sec. 405, 16 (d).

20 *Ibid.*, sec. 407.

21 *Ibid.*, sec. 409.

22 According to sec. 410: "No court shall have jurisdiction to review any Presidential determination or agency action under this Act or any amendment made by this Act."

section (Title V) to the subject. Even here, much of the language was equivocal and nonbinding.[23]

Therefore, Farr believes that the instruments available for the true promotion of religious freedom are limited.[24] One positive aspect was certainly the introduction of the annual report on the status of religious freedom in the world which, according to Farr, helped bring the matter to the attention of State Department officials, traditionally little-inclined to consider religion and religious freedom in their evaluations with regard to US foreign policy.[25]

Some scholars have wondered how much the promotion of religious freedom conflicts with traditional US skepticism on the multilateral protection of human rights.[26] To answer this

[23] Thomas F. Farr, *World of Faith and Freedom. Why International Religious Liberty is Vital to American National Security*, p. 114.

[24] Besides being limited they have also not been used very often: "[...] with few exceptions, those elements of the statute have not been employed to encourage regimes of religious freedom. Although IRFA proponents claimed they sought religious freedom, what they really sought was a U.S. effort to reduce religious persecution. As noted, the absence of persecution is a necessary but insufficient condition for religious freedom, which requires a cultural and political framework to nourish and bound the religious rights of individuals and communities." *Ibid.*

[25] The first report published by the State Department was presented by Robert Seiple in September 1999. Seiple was appointed in March of the same year as Ambassador at Large for International Religious Freedom. During the presentation of the report Seiple stressed how this tool was of fundamental importance for religious minorities around the world and how much it could contribute to the protection of their fundamental rights: "To use a metaphor of a kite, we want to make sure that this new emphasis on this particular human right flies so high that everyone will see it, even those in jail and that this will bring the hope." See *Ambassador Seiple Discusses U.S. Religious Freedom Report: Aim is to Work with Governments Toward Religious Freedom*, quoted in Steven Wales, *Remembering the Persecuted: An Analysis of the International Religious Freedom Act*, p. 595. The 1999 report is also interesting from a scientific point of view because it makes an attempt to classify the different States according to their violations to the right of religious freedom. In the first category we find authoritarian and totalitarian regimes like the Afghanistan of the Taliban, Myanmar, China, Iran, Iraq and Vietnam. In these cases facial example of the right are listed. In the second category we find countries which are hostile to religious minorities and non-recognized religions. Among them Pakistan, Saudi Arabia, Serbia and Sudan. The third category includes countries that tolerate discriminations against religious minorities. Among them: Uzbekistan, Egypt, India and Indonesia. The fourth category includes countries that have specific legal provisions that favour particular religious groups. It is the case of the Russian Federation and Turkey. The last category includes countries that have specific laws against "cults" and "sects," treating them differently from religious groups. It is the case of Belgium, France and Germany. In general the report expressed his favour for diplomatic instruments for the protection of religious freedom over sanctions. It was also criticized for some omissions. Christopher Smith, member of the House of Representatives complained of the lack of reference to persecution against Catholics in Timor East. Nina Shea, at that time member of the U.S. Commission on International Religious Freedom, complained about the lack of specific attention to the violations of the Sudanese government and its complicity with Islamic militias. Other shortcomings were identified in the lack of nomination of the "countries of particular concern" (on which might eventually be imposed sanctions later). The countries were designated later, in October 1999. They were: China, Iran, Myanmar and Sudan. Even if not fully recognized as States there was a mention also to the government of Serbia and to the Talibans. For an analysis of the other reports see Eugenia R. Pastor, "The Flawed Implementation of the International Religious Freedom Act of 1998: A European Perspective," *Brigham Young University Law Review* 3, (2005): pp. 711–746.

[26] According to Mohd Afandi Salleh: "Some question why the United States enacted IRFA as if it is the most important aspect of human rights but, at the same time hesitates and fails to support existing international human rights framework." See Mohd A. Salleh, "The International Religious Freedom Act 1998 and the role of religious movement," p.35.

question, some of the promoters of the International Religious Freedom Act recalled that the objective of the initiative was not to export the US concept of religious freedom expressed in the First Amendment, but to make already-existing international instruments more effective.[27] Peter Danchin was one of the more influential critics of the unilateral US action to promote religious freedom through the International Religious Freedom Act, which, in his interpretation, is a paradigmatic example of unilateralism.[28] Jeremy Gunn has noted the contradictions in this approach, pointing out how it is possible to take actions in promotion of religious freedom that go beyond the "unilateral versus multilateral"[29] dichotomy. However, as Jeremy Gunn states in his response to Peter Danchin, the contribution of multilateral instruments of international law has proven to be particularly weak in protecting religious freedom:

> When the two principal human rights organs of the United Nations are unable to bring to bear any measures or diplomacy against some of the world's worst human rights abusers, Danchin should be asking questions with the same vehemence that he poses when discussing the United States.[30]

The unilateral action of the United States, however, is perceived by some as both an attempt to create a hierarchy of human rights, with the right of religious freedom in a prominent position, and as a true act of imperialism, given the different levels of protection of the rights that currently exist on a global level.[31] From this perspective, a possible critical

27 This may seem to be a paradox for the critics of the International Religious Freedom Act but, according to William Inboden: "Hopefully this Act can also serve as a bulwark against hyper-nationalism. This act is not trying to codify the First Amendment overseas, but rather to build on Article 18 of the Universal Declaration of Human Rights and other international accords. IRFA seeks to strengthen, rather than undermine, international institutions such as the United Nations and the Organization for Security and Cooperation in Europe." See William Inboden, transcription of a speech in Rosalind I.J. Hackett, Mark Silk, David Hoover (eds.), *Religious Persecution as a U.S. Policy Issue, Proceedings of a Consultation held at Trinity College*, p. 14.

28 See Peter G. Danchin, "U.S. Unilateralism and the International Protection of Religious Freedom: The Multilateral Alternative," *Columbia Journal of Transnational Law* 41, no. 1, (2002–2003): pp. 33–136. See also the critiques made by Elizabeth Shakman Hurd in "What's Wrong with Promoting Religious Freedom?", *Foreign Policy*, 12/6/2013, available at: http://mideastafrica.foreignpolicy.com/posts/2013/06/12/whats_wrong_with_promoting_religious_freedom. For a general critique of the unilateral protection and promotion of religious freedom see Lorenzo Zucca, "Prince or Pariah? The Place of Freedom of Religion in a System of International Human Rights," *ReligioWest working paper*, RSCAS 2013/26, April 2013, pp. 1–16.

29 According to Jeremy Gunn multilateral actions for the protection of religious freedom are not exempt from important critiques: "Whereas I agree that the United States should devote more efforts toward improving its own record of participation within the United Nations, Danchin's article gives us a skewed picture in this regard. The principal U.N. organ with the broadest mandate, the Human Rights Commission, has been unable even to agree to criticize China's human rights practices or human rights abuses by the Russians in Chechnia, not to mention its failure to adopt a sound resolution on human rights abuses in Sudan. Perhaps the brightest benefit of the Human Rights Commission has been its sponsoring of the Special Rapporteur for Freedom of Religion and Belief, who continues to issue useful reports within very severe budgetary and political constraints." See Jeremy Gunn, "American Exceptionalism and Globalist Double Standards: A More Balanced Alternative," p. 150.

30 *Ibid.*, p. 151.

31 For this reason some scholars have suggested to include with the mandate of the International Religious Freedom Act the monitoring of the situation of religious freedom within the United States: "IRFA should include a self-assessment of the United States. Though IRFA's mandate extends to every other country in the world (194 countries), neither the State Department nor the Commission can do a self-assessment of

element could be created in relations with some Muslim countries with which – despite some attempts, such as those made in 1990 with the approval of the Cairo Declaration on Human Rights by the Organization of the Islamic Conference[32] – notable differences remain regarding the effective protection of the right. Clear evidence of this difference can be seen in the absence of the right to change religions, which was fundamental in the case of Meriam Ibrahim, a Christian doctor condemned to death in Sudan in May 2014 for apostasy, then released from prison due to international pressure.[33]

Some countries then pointed out that the application of the standards of protection and promotion of the right set out by the International Religious Freedom Act was not uniform for all states, and that some had the perception that the promotion of religious freedom was a smokescreen for the defense and promotion of Christianity alone, or in any case, for a partial notion of religion and religious freedom.[34] Some of these critical points have been dealt with over the past several years by the Obama administration which, as we will see, approved several reforms regarding the US Commission on International Religious Freedom and more generally handled with the subject of promotion of religious freedom with a greater openness to multilateral institutions.

4. The Obama administration reforms

With the election of Barack Obama as President of the United States, a new approach was put into place, both with regard to foreign policy and religious freedom more specifically.

the status of religious freedom within U.S. borders. This failure supports the claim that the United States believes it is superior to the rest of the world on human rights values." See Matthew L. Fore, "Shall Weigh Your God and You: Assessing the Imperialistic Implications of the International Religious Freedom Act in Muslim Countries," *Duke Law Journal* 52, (2002): p. 449.

32 The Organization of the Islamic Conference is an international organization with a permanent delegation at the United Nations. It has as its own goal the protection of the interests and the development of Muslims in the world.

33 Some scholars, among them Matthew Fore, see in the guiding principles of the International Religious Freedom Act an invasion of the sovereignty of Muslim countries: "Religion has played a unique and predominant role in the impulse toward nationhood, and to intervene in a country's handling of its religious practices is to infringe upon a fundamental sovereign power"; moreover in certain Muslim countries it is the very same notion of religious freedom which is criticized because it is understood as a manifestation of US and international understanding of rights: "In Muslim countries like Saudi Arabia, Islam is such a unifying cultural force that group rights may be valued more than the individual rights so often championed in Western society." See Matthew L. Fore, "Shall Weigh Your God and You: Assessing the Imperialistic Implications of the International Religious Freedom Act in Muslim Countries," pp. 436, 438. Also Nadia Marzouki sees in the "imposition" of a certain understanding of religious freedom a problematic aspect of the actions undertaken on the basis of the International Religious Freedom Act. See Nadia Marzouki, *L'Islam, une religion Américaine?* (Paris: Seuil, 2013).

34 See Mohd A. Salleh, "The International Religious Freedom Act 1998 and the role of religious movement," pp. 35–36. As Mohd Afandi Salleh highlights: "Laila al-Marayati, the sole Muslim commissioner of the nine-member US Commission on International Religious Freedom (USCIRF) also criticized the IRFA and claimed the legislation is biased against Islam. In 2002, she issued her dissenting view to the 2001 USCIRF report that did not highlight the situation in Israel and the Occupied Territories in Palestine in the light of IRFA provision. She claims that Israel's denial of Jerusalem holy sites to Palestinian Muslim and Christian was against the provision of IRFA," *ibid.*, p. 37. According to Winnifred Sullivan: "[...] it is clearly not intended to promote freedom of religion. It is intended to promote freedom of a certain kind of religion, religion as it has been shaped by American law and history, religion that has been set apart and contained by the secular state." See Winnifred F. Sullivan, "Exporting Religion. Where the Religious Freedom Act Fails," *Commonweal*, 26/2/1999, p. 11.

Most notable, as previously stated, was the desire to open up to multilateral institutions and initiatives. According to Judd Birdsall, this is precisely the context in which the policies of the Obama administration on the protection and promotion of religious freedom must be framed.[35] This positioning has been repeatedly made evident, beginning with the important Cairo speech of June 2009,[36] particularly with regard to Muslim countries. This change of approach became particularly necessary after the George W. Bush years, which, after the events of September 2001, sometimes saw the manipulation of policies for the promotion of religious freedom.[37] Therefore, according to Judd Birdsall: "Partnership, respect, humility, practicality, and empowering civil society – these Cairo principles have become the hallmark of America's IRF policy under the Obama Administration."[38] Birdsall's analysis – invaluable for its perspective internal to the administration – highlights the perceived need to demonstrate a solid commitment to Christian minorities, which is simultaneously perceived by public opinion and other states as a general commitment to the right of religious freedom.[39]

Other initiatives were the institution of the Forum on Religion and Global Affairs, the Interagency Working Group on Religion and Global Affairs,[40] and the Religion and Foreign Policy Working Group, instituted in October 2011 with the participation of

35 According to Judd Birdsall: "In his words and actions, President Obama has pursued a pragmatic and collaborative diplomacy, guided by a conviction that America strength is best exercised within proper limits and alongside the community of nations." See Judd Birdsall, "Obama and the Drama over International Religious Freedom Policy: An Insider's Perspective," *The Review of Faith and International Affairs* 10, no. 3, (2012): p. 34.

36 See White House, "Remarks by the President on a New Beginning," 4/6/2009, available at: http://goo.gl/XmYyn3. As Judd Birdsall underlines: "The Cairo speech was not only Obama's first major foreign policy address, it was also his first extended treatment of IRF issues. That he highlighted religious freedom as one of seven key concerns in a speech designed to repair US-Islam relations is itself instructive. The Administration has since articulated its commitment to religious freedom in dozens of public statements, but Cairo continues to provide a helpful window on the distinctive elements of the current approach to IRF policy." See Judd Birdsall, "Obama and the Drama over International Religious Freedom Policy. An Insider's Perspective," p. 34. In July 2014 the Obama administration also appointed Shaarik Zafar as Special Representative for the relationships with Muslim communities.

37 This aspect is underlined by Thomas Farr: "These statements exacerbated the already damaging perception in Muslim countries that 'international religious freedom' American-style was a Trojan horse for anti-Islamic forces – a view that meshed quite well with the broader understanding of Western democracy and freedom as inherently godless and therefore enemy of Islam." See Thomas F. Farr, *World of Faith and Freedom. Why International Religious Freedom is Vital to America National Security*, p. 124.

38 Judd Birdsall, "Obama and the Drama over International Religious Freedom Policy: An Insider's Perspective," p. 35.

39 To this extent Judd Birdsall underlines the efforts made by Kurt Donnelly: "[…] an affable and accomplished diplomat and gifted manager, encouraged the staff to pursue new partnerships and explore new projects. Eager to shed a reputation for pro-Christian bias and demonstrate our commitment to advocating on behalf of believers of all stripes, several of us actively engaged a variety of religious groups and interreligious organizations, forging friendships that continue to bolster America's IRF agenda." *Ibid.*

40 Among the different task of these working groups paramount is the one to facilitate the coordination and the collection of information on the efforts of administration toward the different religious groups. As Judd Birdsall underlines: "This Interagency RGA brought together a dozen federal agencies to find the strengths and gaps in our religious engagement and to foster collaboration in addressing those gaps. Our first task was a massive survey, commissioned by the President, of how the federal government was engaging religious groups and faith-based organizations overseas. The RGA forum led the compilation of what would become the State Department's Religious Engagement Report (RER). Using Diplopedia, the Department's internal wiki platform, we received reports from 1,666 embassies, totaling over 600 pages […] The RER revealed a dramatic rise in religious engagement after Cairo, particularly, but not exclusively, with Muslim communities." *Ibid.*, p. 36.

Suzan Johnson Cook, Ambassador at Large for International Religious Freedom. In Judd Birdsall's analysis, the primary commitment of the Office of International Religious Freedom of the State Department is to matters of particular importance in the public debate (e.g., the referendum on minarets in Switzerland,[41] the Pastor Terry Jones[42] incident) and cooperation with certain newly-created institutions such as the Canadian Office for Religious Freedom.[43]

Relations between the Obama administration and the US Commission on International Religious Freedom, however, have been characterized by mutual incomprehension. This was made clear by the events that occurred regarding the reauthorization of the Commission, which was subject to a sunset clause, and therefore needed to be renewed by December 2011.[44] Given its nature as an independent commission, and keeping in mind the strong influence of members appointed by the Republican Party, the US Commission on International Religious Freedom played the role of critic and goad to the administration, and particularly the State Department, at times expressing opinions that were strongly discordant on the situation of religious freedom in some countries. For example, as noted previously, while the US Commission on International Religious Freedom has always been very critical with regard to Saudi Arabia, the State Department has often maintained a very mild, less severe approach. Also given its increasingly frequent conflicts with the State Department, a proposal was floated to decline to reauthorize the US Commission on International Religious Freedom. On December 17, 2011, a few hours before the expected closure, the reauthorization was approved, but with an amendment that imposed severe budget cuts on the Commission.[45] The renewal of the Commission required that the mandate of the commissioners be renewed only once, and contained a new sunset clause that kept the Commission alive until September 30, 2014.[46]

41 In this case there was a referendum proposed on May 1, 2007 by the Union of the Center and the Federal Democratic Union which wanted to ban the construction of minarets. The referendum passed with the consent of 57,5 percent of the voters on November 29, 2009.

42 Terry Jones is the pastor of a Christian church called Dove World Outreach Center; he is also the President of the political group Stand Up America Now. On September 11, 2010 he decided to burn a copy of the Koran. He first decided not to proceed but on April 28, 2012 he effectively burned a copy to protest against the detention of pastor Saeed Adedini in Iran. His initiatives have been followed by several critiques and reactions from the Muslim world.

43 Judd Birdsall highlights the importance of the success against the resolutions on the "defamation of religion" at the United Nations: "During the Bush years, the United States joined European allies in fighting what was effectively an International blasphemy law. The Obama Administration kept up the fight but also sought to collaborate with the OIC to address their underlying concerns. Our diplomats, including Secretary Clinton, acknowledged that discrimination against Muslims in the West is a legitimate concern and showcased America's effort to promote respect for minorities at home and abroad. America's argument, example, and alliance-building ultimately won the day." See Judd Birdsall, "Obama and the Drama over International Religious Freedom Policy. An Insider's Perspective," p. 37.

44 See Nina Shea, "Will the Senate Quietly Kill the U.S. Commission on International Religious Freedom?" *The National Review*, 17/10/2011, available at: http://goo.gl/0ez3Oe.

45 U.S. Congress, H.R. 2867 (112th): *United States Commission on International Religious Freedom Reform and Reauthorization Act of 2011.*

46 This amendment allowed Barack Obama to appoint commissioners closer to the positions of the administration and to those of the Democratic Party. There has been a new authorization until December 11, 2014 with the Continuing Appropriation Resolution 2015 of September 19, 2014. On December 12, 2014, with the vote of the Senate there has been a new authorization until September 30, 2015. See U.S. Congress, H.R. 5816 (113th): *To extend the authorization for the U.S. Commission on International Religious Freedom.*

The need to attribute greater relevance to religion in the realm of foreign policy led to the creation, with the contribution of the State Department, of a new office for relations with religious denominations: the Office for Religious Engagement.[47] The operating methods for the new agency have not yet been fully defined, particularly with regard to coordination with the numerous institutional actors that already crowd the United States scene.[48] An initial analysis shows that the fundamental task of this new agency – which was strongly promoted by the Obama administration and which grew out of the important preparatory work of the Foreign Policy Working Group of the State Department[49] – is not so much dedicated to the promotion of religious freedom in the world as to creating relationships with leaders and religious communities in various countries and sponsoring interreligious and intercultural dialogue. In this respect, it should be remembered that the US Strategy on Religious Leader and Faith Community Engagement defines as fundamental priorities the support of sustainable development and efficient humanitarian aid, the promotion of human rights and specifically the right of religious freedom, and the prevention and resolution of conflicts that could contribute to local and regional instability.[50] Doctrine has been divided with regard to a potential violation of the text of the Establishment Clause of the First Amendment in dialoguing with religious denominations and promoting religious freedom, which the United States put in place in its foreign policy.[51] In the dissenting opinion attached to the report published by the Chicago Council on

47 As Vice-President John Kerry underlined during the presentation of the initiative: "So we need to recognize that in a world where people of all faiths are migrating and mingling like never before, where we are this global community, which we always talk about, we ignore the global impact of religion, in my judgment, at our peril." Kerry also highlights, in particular, the impact on the Muslim world: "And I have talked at length with people like King Abdullah of Saudi Arabia, or even King Abdullah, Prince Ghazi of Jordan, and others who are engaged in interfaith efforts, all of whom recognize that their religion, Islam, has to a large measure been hijacked by people who have no real depth with respect to what the faith in fact preaches, but who interpret it in a way that lead people to conflict and even to violence." John Kerry, "Remarks at the launch of the Office of Faith-Based Community Initiative," 7/8/2013, available at: www.state.gov/secretary/remarks/2013/08/212781.htm.

48 This is another important point underlined by Vice-President John Kerry: "Many of you know that we already have a number of leaders here at the State Department that work on issues related to religion, including our Ambassador-at-Large for International Religious Freedom. And I want to say that I have great respect for and enormous gratitude for their efforts, and these leaders are important and will remain equally as important. I believe that their work will be enhanced by this effort. And the Office of Faith-Based Community Initiatives will grow our ability to be able to reach out to more communities and to create greater understanding between people and countries." *Ibid.*

49 On this issue it has been very influential the working paper titled "*Ensuring Opportunity for Mutual Consent and Collaboration*," published by the working group in October 2012. See Religion and Foreign Policy Working Group, *Ensuring Opportunity for Mutual Consent and Collaboration*, 16/10/2012, available at: http://goo.gl/Mfzz4i

50 See State Department, *U.S. Strategy on Religious Leader and Faith Community Engagement*, available at: www.state.gov/s/fbci/strategy/index.htm.

51 There is still uncertainty on the possibility to apply the Establishment Clause to foreign policy initiatives and actions. This issue is analyzed in an important paragraph of the report published by the Chicago Council on Global Affairs. The authors of the report, even if they admit that the Establishment Clause it is not an obstacle to actions aimed at protecting and promoting freedom of religion abroad, conclude that there is still need to clarify the issue and ask the President to do so: "[...] the Task Force calls upon the President of the United States, advised by executive branch offices and agencies who have studied the problem, to clarify that the Establishment Clause does not bar the United States from engaging religious communities abroad in the conduct of foreign policy, though it does impose constraints on the means that the United States may choose to pursue this engagement." See Scott R. Appleby, Richard Cizik

Global Affairs, "Engaging Religious Communities Abroad: A New Imperative for U.S. Foreign Policy," Jean Bethke Elshtain, Thomas Farr, William Inboden, David Neff, and Timothy Samuel Shah explicitly ask the Obama administration to specify why these actions of the US government do not constitute a violation of the constitutional dictate. According to the authors, a possible restrictive interpretation on this point could harm the interests of the United States in that it does not allow action against religious groups, even in cases where there is a concrete US interest.[52] In response to the dissenting opinion, Frederick Mark Gedicks, Kent Greenawalt, Abner Mikva, George Rupp, and David Saperstein, though recognizing that not all acts of promotion of religious freedom and dialogue with religious communities are prohibited by the Establishment Clause, point out that the constitutional norm poses limits that must be analyzed from time to time in each individual case.[53]

Even during the Obama presidency, despite the sometimes complicated relations with the State Department and the US Commission on International Religious Freedom, interest in the protection and promotion of religious freedom in US foreign policy has had some space. However, some authors have pointed out that, over the past several years, the right of religious freedom has been devolved down to a second-order right, in favor of other rights that have received more enthusiastic promotion by the US government, both with regard to domestic policy and foreign policy.[54] Despite some criticisms of the model of the International Religious Freedom Act, as we will see in subsequent chapters, it has inspired legislative initiatives in several EU countries and in EU institutions in Brussels.

(eds.), *Engaging Religious Communities Abroad: A New Imperative for U.S. Foreign Policy* (Chicago: The Chicago Council on Global Affairs, 2010), p. 65.

52 The authors of the dissenting opinion therefore declare themselves to be against the part of the report which underlines possible conflicts with the Establishment Clause: "We note that this report includes a section on the Establishment Clause only because some members of the American foreign policy establishment – in particular from the State Department and the U.S. Agency for International Development – have interpreted the clause in such a way as to dissuade or prevent them from engaging with religious ideas and actors, even when it is in America's interest to do so." *Ibid.*, p. 84.

53 According to the five authors: "The undersigned members of the Task Force agree that the Establishment Clause does not bar the United States from engaging religion and religious communities abroad in the conduct of its foreign policy. However, the idea that the conduct of U.S. foreign policy is wholly exempt from the Establishment Clause is untenable." *Ibid.*, p. 85.

54 See Mary A. Glendon, "Religious Freedom. A Second Class Right?" *Emory International Law Review* 61, (2012): pp. 971–990. See also Thomas F. Farr, "Obama Administration Sidelines Religious Freedom Policy," *The Washington Post*, 25/6/2010. Thomas Farr was also very critical of the Bush administration in this respect; see Thomas F. Farr, and William L. Saunders jr., "The Bush Administration and America's International Religious Freedom Policy," *Harvard Journal of Law & Public Policy* 32, (2009): pp. 949–970.

References

Appleby, Scott R., and Cizik, Richard (eds.), *Engaging Religious Communities Abroad: A New Imperative for U.S. Foreign Policy* (Chicago: The Chicago Council on Global Affairs, 2010).

Birdsall, Judd, "Obama and the Drama over International Religious Freedom Policy: An Insider's Perspective," *The Review of Faith and International Affairs* 10, no. 3, (2012): pp. 33–41.

Clinton, William J., "Statement on Signing the International Religious Freedom Act of 1998, 27/10/1998, available at: http://goo.gl/8V6LF2.

Danchin, Peter G., "U.S. Unilateralism and the International Protection of Religious Freedom: The Multilateral Alternative," *Columbia Journal of Transnational Law* 41, no. 1, (2002–2003): pp. 33–136.

Farr, Thomas F., "Obama Administration Sidelines Religious Freedom Policy," *The Washington Post*, 25/6/2010.

Farr, Thomas F., and Saunders jr., William L., "The Bush Administration and America's International Religious Freedom Policy," *Harvard Journal of Law & Public Policy* 32, (2009): pp. 949–970.

Farr, Thomas F., *World of Faith and Freedom. Why International Religious Liberty is Vital to American National Security* (New York: Oxford University Press, 2008).

Fore, Matthew L., "Shall Weigh Your God and You: Assessing the Imperialistic Implications of the International Religious Freedom Act in Muslim Countries," *Duke Law Journal* 52, (2002): pp. 423–453.

Glendon, Mary A., "Religious Freedom. A Second Class Right?," *Emory International Law Review* 61, (2012): pp. 971–990.

Gunn, Jeremy, "American Exceptionalism and Globalist Double Standards: A More Balanced Alternative," *Columbia Journal of Transnational Law* 41, (2002–2003): pp. 137–152.

Hertzke, Allen D., *Freeing God's Children. The Unlikely Alliance for Global Human Rights* (Lanham: Rowan & Littlefield, 2004).

Inboden, William, transcription of a speech in Rosalind I.J. Hackett, Mark Silk, and David Hoover (eds.), *Religious Persecution as a U.S. Policy Issue, Proceedings of a Consultation held at Trinity College*, Hartford, 26–27/9/1999.

Kerry, John, "Remarks at the launch of the Office of Faith-Based Community" *Initiative*, 7/8/2013, available at: www.state.gov/secretary/remarks/2013/08/212781.htm.

Marzouki, Nadia, *L'Islam, une religion Américaine?* (Paris: Seuil, 2013).

Pastor, Eugenia R., "The Flawed Implementation of the International Religious Freedom Act of 1998: A European Perspective," *Brigham Young University Law Review* 3, (2005): pp. 711–746.

Religion and Foreign Policy Working Group, *Ensuring Opportunity for Mutual Consent and Collaboration*, 16/10/2012, available at: http://goo.gl/Mfzz4i.

Salleh, Mohd A., "The International Religious Freedom Act of 1998 and the Role of Religious Movement," *Malaysian Journal of History, Politics and Strategic Studies* 38, no. 2, (2011), pp. 27–44.

Shakman Hurd, Elizabeth, in "What's Wrong with Promoting Religious Freedom?," *Foreign Policy*, 12/6/2013, available at: http://mideastafrica.foreignpolicy.com/posts/2013/06/12/whats_wrong_with_promoting_religious_freedom.

Shea, Nina, "Will the Senate Quietly Kill the U.S. Commission on International Religious Freedom?," *The National Review*, 17/10/2011, available at: http://goo.gl/0ez3Oe.

State Department, *U.S. Strategy on Religious Leader and Faith Community Engagement*, available at: www.state.gov/s/fbci/strategy/index.htm.

Sullivan, Winnifred F., "Exporting Religion. Where the Religious Freedom Act Fails," *Commonweal*, 26/2/1999.

Wales, Steven, "Remembering the Persecuted: An Analysis of the International Religious Freedom Act," *Houston Journal of International Law* 24, no. 3 (2002): pp. 579–648.

White House, "Remarks by the President on a New Beginning," 4/6/2009, available at: http://goo.gl/XmYyn3.

Zucca, Lorenzo, "Prince or Pariah? The Place of Freedom of Religion in a System of International Human Rights," *ReligioWest working paper*, RSCAS 2013/26, April 2013, pp. 1–16.

Part II

Religious freedom in the external relations of the European Union

4 European Union law and religious freedom

1. European Union law and fundamental rights

Before analyzing the role of religious freedom in the external relations of the European Union, and the influence of the International Religious Freedom Act upon it, it seems necessary to note developments related to the protection of fundamental rights by European supranational institutions. This is the context for the development of policies that protect and promote religious freedom.[1]

The European Economic Community was established for the pursuit of economic and commercial ends; there is therefore no explicit reference to the aspect of fundamental rights. The principal political interest of the founding countries was to create a single internal market. The founding countries saw this as a powerful political incentive to help create synergies and avoid further divisions among the European countries; the protection of human rights was not one of the primary objectives of the European Economic Community. The issue was addressed explicitly only starting in the 1970s, when a series of rulings of the Court of Justice of the European Community began the work of recognizing the basic human rights that jurisprudence considered to be an integral part of the EU system.[2] Subsequently, through the approval of the Single European Act, human rights formally became a part of the system of rights protection set out by the treaties. With the Treaties of Maastricht and Amsterdam, human rights became fundamental values of the European Union,[3] resulting

1 For an introduction to the topic see Ronan McCrea, *Religion and the Public Order of the European Union* (Oxford: Oxford University Press, 2010). See also François Foret, *Religion and Politics in the European Union. The Secular Canopy* (Cambridge: Cambridge University Press, 2015).

2 See, among the others, the decision of the Court of Justice of the European Union *Van Gend & Loss v. Nederlandse Administratie der Belastingen* (C-26/62), 5/2/1963; *Stauder v. City of Ulm* (C-29/69), 12/11/1969; *Internationale Handelgesellschaft v. Einfuhrund* (c-11/70), 17/12/1970. Other specific judgments of the Court of Justice have had an important impact on the development of a human rights culture within the EU. See *Rutili v. Ministero dell'Interno* (C-36/75), 28/10/1975; *Panellinia Omospondia Syllogon Prosspikou v. Dimotiki Etairia Pliroforissis and Sotirios Kouvelas and Nicolaos Avdellas and others* (C-260/89), 18/6/1991. There are also important decision with a direct impact on religion, see *Van Duyn v. United Kingdom* (C-41/74), 4/12/1974 (concerning the denial of entry into the UK to a member of Scientology) and *Prais v. Council of the European Communities* (C-130/75), 27/10, 1976 (concerning a public competition undertaken by a person of Jewish faith). For a general analysis of these judgments see M. Parisi, *Affermazione di principi in materia religiosa nella giurisprudenza delle Corti di Strasburgo e del Lussembrugo*, in G. Macrì, M. Parisi, V. Tozzi, *Diritto e Religione* (Salerno: Plectica, 2011): pp. 121–126.

3 This shift in relevance for human rights within the European Union is underlined by Marco Ventura which also links them to parallel developments within the system of the Council of Europe: "In the period

in the establishment of a procedure to suspend the rights of a Member State in the event of severe and persistent violations. It also established compliance with a minimum standard of respect for human rights as a prerequisite to begin the procedure for European Union membership. The EU Charter of Fundamental Rights was proclaimed on December 7, 2000,[4] then proclaimed again in a version adopted on December 12, 2007 in Strasbourg. Under Article 6, with the entry into force of the Treaty of Lisbon, the Charter assumed the same legal status as the Treaties (with a special regime for Poland and the United Kingdom, in accordance with the protocols annexed to the Treaty), and attributed particular importance to six fundamental principles: dignity (Arts. 1–5), freedoms (Arts. 6–19), equality (Arts. 20–26), solidarity (Arts. 27–38), citizen's rights (Arts. 39–46), and justice (Arts. 47–50). The legal value of the Charter of Rights, however, is also connected to the prospect of the EU's adherence to the European Convention of Human Rights, set out under paragraph 2, Article 6 of the Treaty on European Union. From this point of view, it will be important to see which forms of coordination will be used to interpret the various norms protecting religious freedom.

In the face of the continuous development of the role of human rights in the EU system, which takes place above all through jurisprudence, some scholars, politicians, and representatives of religious groups themselves have maintained (and some of them still maintain) that the various national regulations regarding the relationship between church and state and the protection of religious freedom should and could be preserved from the impact of a legal system such as that of the European Union, which is perceived as overly favorable to an individualistic reading of human rights, at times detached from its social and collective component.[5] Today, as we will see, it is this social, political, and legal reality that is calling into question an overly literal interpretation of norms intended only to protect the regulatory regimes present in individual countries. Recent developments, in fact, indicate that these same religious groups are increasingly requesting greater engagement from the institutions of the Union in protection of religious freedom, particularly in the context of the external relations of the European Union.[6]

from the Treaty of Maastricht (1992) to the Treaty of Amsterdam (1997), the European Union added to the language of the single market the language of political goals, common constitutional traditions, non-discrimination, and fundamental rights. Human rights and freedom were no longer the sole preserve of the Council of Europe, the European Convention of Human Rights, and the Strasbourg Court. The European Union was stepping in." See Marco Ventura, "Dynamic Law and Religion in Europe. Acknowledging Change. Choosing Change," *ReligioWest EUI working paper*, RSCAS 91, (2013): p. 14.

4 The decision which would bring to the elaboration of the Charter was taken in Koln by the European Council on June 3–4, 1999.

5 See Marta Cartabia, "L'ora dei diritti fondamentali nell'Unione Europea," in Marta Cartabia (eds.), *I diritti in azione. Universalità e pluralismo dei diritti fondamentali nelle Corti europee* (Bologna: Il Mulino, 2007), pp. 13–66.

6 Marco Ventura reconstructs the different steps of this evolution by linking them to the regulation of the labor market through the law of the European Union and the logic of the common market: "To what extent could the free market invade culture, society and thus religion? How far could Europe follow, regardless of national specificities and identities? What was still up to individual States? The economy challenged the institutional architecture as well as the political process. The market imposed its mindset. No longer 'protected' by the external enemy of international communism, European cohesion around liberal capitalism, and the role of religion in such a pattern, were challenged." See Marco Ventura, "Dynamic Law and Religion in Europe. Acknowledging Change. Choosing Change," p. 15.

2. Law and policy on religious freedom of the European Union: Article 17 of the Treaty of Lisbon

The developments of the law of the European Union indicate to us the progressive interest of EU institutions in both human rights and religion. Before analyzing the role of the latter, and the right of religious freedom in the context of the external relations of the EU, we must discuss some aspects particularly related to the role of EU institutions in the regulation of religion. EU law recently introduced significant innovations on the protection of religious freedom. First, Article 10 of the Charter of Fundamental Rights contains a specific regulatory provision on the protection of religious freedom. According to Article 10 of the Charter:

> Everyone has the right to freedom of thought, conscience and religion. This right includes freedom to change religion or belief and freedom, either alone or in community with others and in public or in private, to manifest religion or belief, in worship, teaching, practice and observance.

The actual scope of the provision has yet to be established. This will depend in particular on how the EU institutions will wish to make use of the principle, especially the Luxembourg Court of Justice.[7] Outside of "ambiguities"[8] or interpretive difficulties, which persist in any case, what seems undeniable is that there has been "a particularly complex network of relations and influences"[9] between EU law and religion. In fact, there are numerous areas of interaction between EU law and religion: norms on citizenship, anti-discrimination law, norms on immigration and the right to asylum,[10] and the recent initiatives on the promotion and protection of religious freedom in the external actions of the EU, which are the subject of this work.[11] The Court of Justice of the European Union must rule both on events that, even if not directly related to the interpretation of norms on religious freedom, are bearers of important implications for the legal treatment of religious groups and also, most recently, on a case relating to the legal notion of "religious persecution," in which it gave a very extensive interpretation of the notion of religious freedom.[12]

7 There will be the need to verify how supranational and national sources of law will be coordinated, especially as far as EU and the law of the ECHR are concerned. See Roberto Mazzola, "Confessioni, organizzazioni filosofiche e associazioni religiose nell'Unione Europea tra speranze disilluse e problemi emergenti," *Stato, Chiese e Pluralismo confessionale*, January 2014, pp. 1–14.

8 *Ibid.*

9 *Ibid.*, p. 5.

10 See also Sergio Carrera, Joanna Parkin, "The Place of Religion in European Union Law and Policy. Competing Approaches and Actors inside the European Commission," *Religare working paper n. 1*, (September 2010).

11 I have already dealt previously with this topic. See Pasquale Annicchino, "Freedom of Religion or Belief in the Foreign Policy of the European Union. Much Ado About Nothing?" in Mary A. Glendon and Rafael Alvira (eds.), *Religion and Civil Society: The Changing Faces of Religion and Secularity* (New York: Georg Olms, 2014), pp. 115–129 and Pasquale Annicchino, "Is the European Union Going Deep on Democracy and Religious Freedom?" *The Review of Faith and International Affairs* 12, no. 3, (2014): pp. 33–40.

12 Court of Justice of the European Union, *The Federal Republic of Germany v. Y and Z* (C-71/11), (C-99/11), 5/9/2012 (concerning the request for asylum of two Pakistani nationals for reasons of religious persecution).

Despite these recent developments, which indicate the steady influence of EU law on the regulation of religion, there is not yet a unanimous doctrinal position on the actual competence of EU institutions in this matter. The current formulation of Article 17 of the Lisbon Treaty reflects well the content of Declaration 11, annexed to the 1996 Treaty of Amsterdam, which attempted to prevent the interference of EU law on topics related to the legal status of religious denominations.[13]

According to Article 17 of the Treaty of Lisbon:

> 1) The Union respects and does not prejudice the status under national law of churches and religious associations or communities in the Member States. 2) The Union equally respects the status under national law of philosophical and non-confessional organizations. 3) Recognizing their identity and their specific contribution, the Union shall maintain an open, transparent and regular dialogue with these churches and organizations.

As previously noted, the norm is the result of a long and complicated process that involved European churches in difficult policy negotiations aimed at obtaining a "special protection clause for the legal status assured to them up to now by various national legal systems."[14] This need arose from the fear that the activism of European institutions could threaten a national sphere of influence perceived as exclusive, that is to say, by the "need to thus ensure that those spaces of freedom and autonomy (and, perhaps, of privilege) remain unchanged."[15] The doctrine has been heavily questioned over the years with regard to the legal scope and interpretation of the norm. If on the one hand the norm could take on a static aspect, with its promise of "respecting the national statuses" of various religious, philosophical, and non-denominational organizations, on the other it certainly introduces a dynamic element through its anticipation of a dialogue between these organizations and EU institutions.[16] From this perspective, paragraph 3 of the provision leaves open in any case important questions concerning its interpretation.

The three paragraphs of the provision are to be interpreted in a coordinated manner, since only a proper interpretation and application of the first two paragraphs can lead to the identification of the subjects for dialogue set out under paragraph 3 of Article 17. One response, perhaps partial, to these questions can be found in the recent recommendation of the European Ombudsman on the appeal of the European Humanist Federation against the Commission[17] on the methods of conducting the dialogue under Article 17 of the

13 See Marco Ventura, "Dynamic Law and Religion in Europe. Acknowledging Change. Choosing Change," and also Marco Ventura, "The Changing Civil Religion of Secular Europe," *George Washington International Law Review* 41, no. 4, (2010): pp. 947–961.

14 Angelo Licastro, *Unione Europea e "status" delle confessioni religiose. Fra tutela dei diritti umani fondamentali e salvaguardia delle identità costituzionali* (Milano: Giuffrè, 2014), p. 123.

15 *Ibid.*

16 See, among the others, Thomas Jansen, "Europe and Religions: The Dialogue between the European Commission and Churches or Religious Communities," *Social Compass* 47, no. 1, (2000): pp. 103–112.

17 Decision of the European Ombudsman against the European Commission on article 17 of the Treaty on the Functioning of the European Union, January 2013 (app. 2097/2011/RA). For a comment on the decision see Pasquale Annicchino, "Il Dialogo con i gruppi religiosi e le organizzazioni non confessionali del Diritto dell'Unione europea: a proposito di una recente pronuncia del Mediatore europeo," *Quaderni di Diritto e Politica Ecclesiastica* 3, (2013): pp. 747–756 and also Pasquale Annicchino, "Religion and EU Institutions," *Ecclesiastical Law Journal* 15, no. 3, (2013): pp. 326–331.

Treaty of Lisbon and the subsequent Guidelines approved by the cabinet of Commission President Barroso.[18] In this recommendation, the European Ombudsman reviewed elements of "bad administration" in the Commission's management of relations with religious denominations and philosophical or non-denominational organizations for failing to organize a seminar proposed by the European Humanist Federation. The recommendation of the European Ombudsman is further confirmation of the importance of EU law for various national regulations and its substantial impact on church and state relations on a national level. Angelo Licastro summarizes it well:

> Even the most nostalgic proponents (if any remain) of an "autarchic religious law" must clearly face and come to terms with the unifying or uniform effect exercised by European law and jurisprudence (directly or indirectly) on national law, and therefore also the areas of those laws dedicated to the governance of religion.[19]

Naturally, the intervention of EU institutions can at times exceed a responsible implementation of the limits imposed by the treaties, but it seems fundamentally unrealistic to continue to argue that EU law is relegated to the margins in the debate on the regulation of religion. This is all the more true when those same EU institutions act to protect the promotion and protection of religious freedom, with the support and upon the request of numerous churches and religious groups, as occurs in the external relations of the Union, and thus in the field of European foreign policy. As Marco Ventura said, it can be maintained, paradoxically, that Article 17 of the Treaty of Lisbon: "represented a fundamental contribution to the birth of a true religious law of the European Union."[20]

The perspective of the external relations of the EU then, which is the visual angle from which this work views relations between EU law and religious freedom, offers a new and unprecedented perspective on the challenge to the role of EU institutions in the development of a policy, and therefore a simultaneous law, on religion. This perspective is useful in understanding the influence of the US institutional and regulatory model on the European Union and on other countries who have made the promotion and protection of religious freedom a specific policy objective.

18 European Commission, *Guidelines on the Implementation of Article 17 by the European Commission*, available at: http://ec.europa.eu/bepa/pdf/dialogues/guidelines-implementation-art-17.pdf.

19 Angelo Licastro, *Unione Europea e "status" delle confessioni religiose. Fra tutela dei diritti umani fondamentali e salvaguardia delle identità costituzionali*, p. 219.

20 Marco Ventura, "L'articolo 17 TFUE come fondamento del diritto e della politica ecclesiastica dell'Unione Europea," *Quaderni di Diritto e Politica Ecclesiastica*, 2, (2014): p. 302.

References

Annicchino, Pasquale, "Freedom of Religion or Belief in the Foreign Policy of the European Union. Much Ado About Nothing?" in Mary A. Glendon, and Rafael Alvira (eds.), *Religion and Civil Society: The Changing Faces of Religion and Secularity* (New York: Georg Olms, 2014), pp. 115–129.

Annicchino, Pasquale, "Is the European Union Going Deep on Democracy and Religious Freedom?" *The Review of Faith and International Affairs* 12, no. 3, (2014): pp. 33–40.

Annicchino, Pasquale, "Il Dialogo con i gruppi religiosi e le organizzazioni non confessionali del Diritto dell'Unione europea: a proposito di una recente pronuncia del Mediatore europeo," *Quaderni di Diritto e Politica Ecclesiastica* 3, (2013): pp. 747–756.

Annicchino, Pasquale, "Religion and EU Institutions," *Ecclesiastical Law Journal* 15, no. 3, (2013): pp. 326–331.

Cartabia, Marta, "L'ora dei diritti fondamentali nell'Unione Europea," in Marta Cartabia (eds.), *I diritti in azione. Universalità e pluralismo dei diritti fondamentali nelle Corti europee* (Bologna: Il Mulino, 2007), pp. 13–66.

Carrera, Sergio, and Parkin Joanna, "The Place of Religion in European Union Law and Policy. Competing Approaches and Actors inside the European Commission," *Religare working paper n. 1*, (September 2010).

Foret, François, *Religion and Politics in the European Union. The Secular Canopy* (Cambridge: Cambridge University Press, 2015).

Jansen, Thomas, "Europe and Religions: The Dialogue between the European Commission and Churches or Religious Communities," *Social Compass* 47, no. 1, (2000): pp. 103–112.

Licastro, Angelo, *Unione Europea e "status" delle confessioni religiose. Fra tutela dei diritti umani fondamentali e salvaguardia delle identità costituzionali* (Milano: Giuffrè, 2014).

McCrea, Ronan, *Religion and the Public Order of the European Union* (Oxford: Oxford University Press, 2010).

Parisi, Marco, *Affermazione di principi in materia religiosa nella giurisprudenza delle Corti di Strasburgo e del Lussembrugo*, in G. Macrì, M. Parisi, V. Tozzi, *Diritto e Religione* (Salerno: Plectica, 2011), pp. 121–126.

Ventura, Marco, "Dynamic Law and Religion in Europe. Acknowledging Change. Choosing Change," *ReligioWest EUI working paper*, RSCAS 91, (2013): pp. 947–961.

Roberto, Mazzola, "Confessioni, organizzazioni filosofiche e associazioni religiose nell'Unione Europea tra speranze disilluse e problemi emergenti," *Stato, Chiese e Pluralismo confessionale*, January 2014, pp. 1–14.

Ventura, Marco, "The Changing Civil Religion of Secular Europe," *George Washington International Law Review* 41, no. 4, (2010): pp. 947–961.

5 Protection and promotion of religious freedom in the external relations of the European Union

1. Human rights in the external relations of the European Union

The role of the right to religious freedom in relations between EU institutions and religious groups has been a focus of interest to scholars for many years.[1] It is only recently that this focus has shifted to the analysis of the new legal sources that govern the EU's role in protecting and promoting religious freedom in its external relations. This development was made possible by the approval of the Treaty of Lisbon and the creation of institutions responsible for the pursuit of a true EU foreign policy.[2] As an international organization with its own legal personality distinct from those of its Member States, the EU actually has the capacity to establish relations with other states and international organizations.

In this context, the EU prepared an "external action plan" whose novelty, as Alberto Fabbri points out,

> [...] consists precisely in the new face that the Union presents on the international scene, the bearer of a new order to aspire to, proposing the creation of a peace

1 See Ronan McCrea, *Religion and the Public Order of the European Union*.

2 Since 1993 the European Union within the framework of the Maastricht Treaty has begun to explore the dimension of its external action. The Treaty foresaw a structure based on three pillars: the European Community, the Common Foreign and Security Policy, Justice and Home Affairs. The dimension of external affairs had therefore a clear inter-governmental dimension. The Treaty of Lisbon has changed this structure and with article 27 creates the new European External Action Service. According to article 27 of the Treaty: "1. The High Representative of the Union for Foreign Affairs and Security Policy, who shall chair the Foreign Affairs Council, shall contribute through his proposals towards the preparation of the common foreign and security policy and shall ensure implementation of the decisions adopted by the European Council and the Council. 2. The High Representative shall represent the Union for matters relating to the common foreign and security policy. He shall conduct political dialogue with third parties on the Union's behalf and shall express the Union's position in international organisations and at international conferences. 3. In fulfilling his mandate, the High Representative shall be assisted by a European External Action Service. This service shall work in cooperation with the diplomatic services of the Member States and shall comprise officials from relevant departments of the General Secretariat of the Council and of the Commission as well as staff seconded from national diplomatic services of the Member States. The organisation and functioning of the European External Action Service shall be established by a decision of the Council. The Council shall act on a proposal from the High Representative after consulting the European Parliament and after obtaining the consent of the Commission." The European External Action Service therefore does not substitute national diplomatic services but works in cooperation with them. For an introduction with particular focus on the dimension of religious freedom see Pasquale Annicchino, *Freedom of Religion or Belief in the Foreign Policy of the European Union. Much Ado About Nothing?*.

> that allows the development of democracy, the state of law, and respect for human rights.[3]

The right of religious freedom then becomes, as we will see, an important tool for the European Union through concrete means such as "the insertion of 'human rights clauses' into agreements with non-EU countries, to create a policy that incentivizes achievement of levels of democracy in countries interested in collaboration, so that the Union can initiate a relationship with them."[4] The European Union has begun to equip itself with several legal instruments that can be used to pursue the objective of full development of human rights – and therefore the right of religious freedom – in its bilateral and multilateral relations. As we will see, it has done so partially inspired by the US model analyzed above, and influenced by it.

2. Guidelines on religious freedom

The European Union has explicitly committed itself to the promotion and protection of religious freedom in the context of its external action. This political decision can be attributed to multiple factors. Out of these we can identify at least three: the persecution and violence suffered by numerous Christian communities in various parts of the world,[5] constitutional transitions in the countries of the former Soviet bloc, and the rise of movements tied to political Islam. These factors have certainly evoked a path of reflection among scholars and those in the political and diplomatic communities, in connection with a new primacy of religion in the dynamics of the comprehension and development of international relations.[6]

After a series of violent attacks against Christian communities around the world in January 2011, the European Parliament issued a resolution asking the High Representative for Foreign Affairs and Security Policy to institute a "permanent capacity within the human rights directorate of the European External Action Service to monitor the situation of governmental and societal restrictions on religious freedom and related rights, and to report

3 Alberto Fabbri, *Unione europea e fenomeno religioso. Alcune valutazioni di principio* (Torino: Giappichelli, 2012), p. 14.

4 *Ibid.*, p. 15

5 Pope Francis has underlined how this is an increasing global trend: "The persecuted Christians are a concern that touches me very deeply as a pastor. I know a lot about persecutions but it doesn't seem prudent to talk about them here so I don't offend anyone. But in some places it is prohibited to have a Bible or teach the catechism or wear a cross [...] What I would like to be clear on is one thing, I am convinced that the persecution against Christians today is stronger than in the first centuries of the Church. Today there are more Christian martyrs than in that period. And, it's not because of fantasy, it's because of the numbers." Catholic News Agency, "Full Text of Pope Francis interview with 'La Vanguardia'", 13/6/2014, available at: www.catholicnewsagency.com/news/pope-francis-interview-with-la-vanguardia---full-text-45430/.

6 This issue is well analyzed from a diplomatic perspective by Pasquale Ferrara: "The global re-birth of religions represents one of the key aspects of the process, currently ongoing across the globe, of identity re-definition; such a process involves individuals, communities, institutions and social structures in general [...] In particular, the discipline of international relations and diplomatic practice can no longer ignore the virtues and the behaviours of a large number of faith-based communities spread around the world. This raises a fundamental question: is this new religious dynamicity a problem or potential asset in the field of international relations?" See Pasquale Ferrara, *Global Religions and International Relations. A Diplomatic Perspective* (New York: Palgrave, 2014), p. 10.

annually to Parliament".[7] The same requests were advanced by numerous churches, religious groups and non-governmental organizations in Brussels. Among others, the Commission of the Bishops' Conferences of the European Community and the Conference of European Churches emphasized how, in their opinion, the European External Action Service could play an important role in the protection and promotion of religious freedom.[8]

Also determinant was the political action of some members of European Parliament who, inspired by the work of the US Commission on International Religious Freedom, in 2009 started to investigate the possibility of a European action.[9] It would obviously be impossible to replicate on a European level the particular US experience and structure,[10] but as Denis De Jong recalls, the desire of some European parliamentarians and the personal relations they established with US officials significantly facilitated the European initiative.[11]

One feature of the action of the members of the European Parliament is the convergence of interests, in this case, among parliamentarians connected to the European People's Party and those connected to secular bodies or secularists, in line with the positions of the European Platform for Secularism in Europe.[12]

7 European Parliament, *Resolution of 20 January 2011 on the situation of Christians in the context of freedom of religion*, 20/1/2011, available at: www.europarl.europa.eu/sides/getDoc.do?pubRef=-//EP//TEXT+TA+P7-TA-2011-0021+0+DOC+XML+V0//EN.

8 COMECE, *Religious Freedom. Pillar of the Human Rights Policy in the External Relations* (Brussels: Comece, 2010). The Commission has also produced a report where the actions for the protection and promotion of religious freedom of the European Parliament and of the European External Action Service are analyzed. See COMECE, *A Compilation Report on Religious Freedom at the European Parliament and the European External Action Service (EEAS)*, January–September 2012.

9 As Denis De Jong has argued: "I started with the organization in 2009, of a special 'event' on freedom of religion or belief and EU's external policies. With the help of the Spanish Presidency and a number of representatives from Member States' Foreign Offices, we engaged in a lively debate on the need for EU guidelines on the protection of freedom of religion or belief." See Dennis De Jong, "The Role of the European Parliament in Helping to Protect Freedom of Religion or Belief via the EU's External Relations," in Pasquale Annicchino (eds.), *Freedom of Religion or Belief in Foreign Policy. Which one?* (Florence: EUI University Press, 2013), pp. 44–45. The idea of a transatlantic partnership has been also advanced by Knox Thames, former Director of Policy of the US Commission on International Religious Freedom. See Knox Thames, "Forging a Trans-Atlantic Partnership on Religious Freedom," *The Review of Faith and International Affairs* 12, no. 3, (2014): pp. 1–8.

10 The process is well described by Dennis De Jong: "Part of this process was the elaboration of a working paper by the group of like-minded MEPs to be transmitted to the EEAS. It contained a number of recommendations for the working methods of the EEAS, as well as an annex with the main areas of developments of concern. In that respect, our paper was in a way comparable to the annual reports of the U.S. Commission on International Religious Freedom." See Dennis De Jong, "The Role of the European Parliament in Helping to Protect Freedom of Religion or Belief via the EU's External Relations," p. 45.

11 Denis De Jong stresses in particular the role of Leonard Leo, at that time Chair of the U.S. Commission on International Religious Freedom: "[…] it was important that during his visit to the European Parliament the then Chair of USCIRF, Mr. Leonard Leo, told me that USCIRF was looking to network like ours. For example, in the German Bundestag a similar network exists and USCIRF considers this to be one of their counterparts, as an official Commission like in the USA does not exist anywhere in Europe. It would be only logical to liaise in a comparable manner as European Parliament-network with USCIRF." *Ibid.*

12 For example Sophie In't Veldt, at that time Chair of the European Platform for Secularism in Europe, declared: "The EU should more actively seek the protection of religious minorities against violence or persecution. The EU should promote secular democracy, as the best guarantee of freedom of religion or belief – including non-religious stances – as an individual fundamental right for all citizens." See European Platform for Secularism in Europe, "EU to Defend Freedom of Religion and Secular Democracy in External Policies," 7/11/2011, available at: https://epthinktank.eu/2013/05/06/freedom-of-religion-and-belief-in-external-eu-policies/

The EU's interest in this type of action was also confirmed by the approval of the Strategic Framework for Human Rights, a document that identifies the priorities of the Union in the field of human rights through the European Union Council, which identifies three distinct types of possible actions for the Union:

a) Develop public EU Guidelines on Freedom of Religion or Belief (FoRB) building upon existing instruments and documents, recalling key principles and containing clearly defined priorities and tools for the promotion of FoRB worldwide;
b) Present EU initiatives at the UN level on freedom of religion or belief, including resolutions at General Assembly and Human Rights Council;
c) Promote initiatives at the level of OSCE and the Council of Europe and contribute to better implementation of commitments in the area of Freedom of Religion or Belief.[13]

These general objectives in the Strategic Framework for Human Rights were the basis of the draft of the text of the Guidelines of the EU Foreign Affairs Council, approved in June 2013.

3. Fundamental principles of the actions of the European Union in the context of the Guidelines

The text approved by the Foreign Affairs Council on June 24, 2013, entitled *EU Guidelines on the Promotion and Protection of Freedom of Religion or Belief*,[14] defines the principles and methods available to the European External Action Service for the protection of religious freedom. First, it imposes a consideration on the type of legal source and its consequent efficacy. Unlike a directive or a regulation, the Guidelines are not a legally binding instrument, but are limited to offering some political aims that European officials should consider in their actions. This immediately indicates a clear and significant difference from other similar experiences, particularly the US experience. Although lacking binding legal efficacy, the Guidelines offer important jumping-off points and useful elements for an analysis of the relationship between the EU and religious freedom. The reasons for European action lie first of all in the universal scope of the right of religious freedom and the frequent violation of this right by state and non-state actors.[15] With regard to the protection and promotion of religious freedom, the European Union should aspire to the principles of "universality, indivisibility, interrelatedness, and interdependence of human rights."[16] Later, paragraph 5 of the Guidelines specifically urges Member Countries to respect religious freedom within their own borders as well.

The Guidelines list other principles of fundamental importance for their application. For example, it excludes the EU's alignment with a specific religious denomination,[17] indicating a preference for a neutral approach. It also describes the notion of religious freedom that is

13 Council of the European Union, *EU Strategic Framework and Action Plan of Human Rights and Democracy*, 25/6/2012, p. 18, available at: www.consilium.europa.eu/uedocs/cms_data/docs/pressdata/EN/foraff/131181.pdf.

14 Council of the European Union, *EU Guidelines on the Promotion and Protection of Freedom of Religion or Belief*, 24/6/2013, available at: https://eeas.europa.eu/sites/eeas/files/137585.pdf.

15 *Ibid*., par. 3.

16 *Ibid*., par. 4.

17 At par. 7 it is specified how: "[...] the EU focuses on the right of individuals, to believe, and, alone or in community with others, to freely manifest their beliefs. The EU does not consider the merits of the

the theoretical linchpin of the text, derived from sources of international law: Article 18 of the Universal Declaration of Human Rights and Article 1 of the International Covenant on Civil and Political Rights. These sources yield the two fundamental sources of law:

> *a)* the freedom to have or not to have or adopt (which includes the right to change) a religion or belief of one's choice, and *b)* the freedom to manifest one's religion or belief, individually or in community with others, in public or private, through worship, observance, practice and teaching.[18]

The Guidelines state that the terms "religion" and "conviction" must be understood in the broad sense, not limited to traditional religions only,[19] and that any limitations to the right to manifest one's own religion or conviction must be assessed according to a stringent criterion of proportionality.[20]

The second part of the Guidelines defines the operational principles at the basis of EU action. It reiterates, first, the universal character of the right of religious freedom and its individual and collective nature. The third section of the second part, almost to signal deference to the states, highlights the priority role of the state entity in the protection of religious freedom. The presence of this section in the text of the Guidelines is probably due to the concerns of those states, which, in the Council on Foreign Affairs, feared the excessive activism of the EU in this regard at the expense of national prerogatives.[21]

The fourth section of the second part emphasizes that religious freedom is to be interpreted in connection with the other fundamental rights, and in particular, with regard to the European External Action Service, with other Guidelines produced that provide instructions on this topic.[22] From this perspective, it will be particularly interesting to analyze coordination with the Guidelines that protect lesbian, gay, bisexual, transgender, and intersexual persons, also approved on June 24, 2013.[23]

4. The Guidelines and priority areas and instruments of action

Section B of the second part of the Guidelines identifies the priority action areas for the protection and promotion of religious freedom in the external relations of the European

different religions or belief, or the lack thereof, but ensures that the right to believe or not to believe is upheld." *Ibid.*, par. 7.

18 *Ibid.*, par. 9.

19 *Ibid.*, par. 11.

20 Par. 14 reminds how: "These limitations must be in accordance with international standards and must be strictly interpreted. Limitations for other reasons, such as national security, are not permitted." *Ibid.*, par. 14.

21 *Ibid.*, par. 21, 22, 23, 24.

22 *Ibid.*, par. 27: "In dealing with possible violations, use will be made of existing EU human rights guidelines, notably the guidelines on the promotion and protection of rights of the child, on violence against women and girls, and combating all forms of discrimination against them, on human rights defenders, on torture and on the death penalty, as well as the forthcoming EU guidelines on the enjoyment of all human rights by LGBTI persons, and on freedom of expression on line and off line."

23 Council of the European Union, *Guidelines to Promote and Protect the Enjoyment of all Human Rights by Lesbian, Gay, Bisexual, Transgender and Intersex (LGBTI)*, 24/6/2013, available at: www.consilium.europa.eu/uedocs/cms_data/docs/pressdata/en/foraff/137584.pdf. For a first analysis of the guidelines see Pasquale Annicchino, "The New Guidelines on Freedom of Religion and LGBTI Rights in the External Action of the European Union," *European Human Rights Law Review*, 6, (2013): pp. 624–630.

Union. The first priority action area concerns religiously-motivated violence by state or non-state actors.[24] In the case of religiously-motivated violence, the European Union is called upon to issue a public condemnation[25] and demand that those responsible be brought to justice.[26] Other measures concern the request, to be submitted to the relevant state, for legislative initiatives aimed at prohibiting the public encouragement of religious violence under Article 20, paragraph 2 of the International Covenant on Civil and Political Rights.[27]

Another priority action identified by the Guidelines concerns freedom of expression, identified as a right strongly connected with religious freedom[28]: some cases typical of this conflict can be seen, for example, in the prohibition on the distribution of religious material or the limitation of freedom of speech or opinion. When these types of events occur, paragraph 32 of the Guidelines provides detailed guiding principles for European diplomatic action, with the caveat that, in any case, the religion itself cannot be exempt from criticism, therefore expressing a need for a broad protection of the right of free expression.[29] This point takes on particular importance if we consider the repeated initiatives presented at the United Nations over the past several years introducing resolutions against blasphemy.[30]

The third priority action area identified by the Guidelines concerns the promotion of respect for diversity and tolerance. Particular attention is given to the role of the educational system, which is assigned primary importance in this context.[31]

The fourth priority action area concerns the fight against discrimination, both against individuals due to their religious faith or convictions, and against communities *qua* religious communities, and as minority expressions within a religious community. In this case as well, paragraph 37 sets out specific actions that the European Union can take in support of the fight against discrimination.[32]

24 Several examples are offered: "[...] killing, execution, disappearance, torture, sexual violence, abductions and inhuman degrading treatment." See Council of the European Union, *EU Guidelines on the Promotion and Protection of Freedom of Religion or Belief*, par. 29.

25 *Ibid.*, par. 30.

26 *Ibid.*

27 *Ibid.*, par. 30 e): "Demand the national adoption of laws that prohibit public advocacy of religious hatred that constitutes incitement to discrimination, hostility and violence." According to article 20, 2 of the International Covenant on Civil and Political Rights: "Any advocacy of national, racial or religious hatred that constitutes incitement to discrimination, hostility or violence shall be prohibited by law."

28 *Ibid.*, par. 31: "Freedom of religion or belief and the freedom of expression are interdependent, interrelated and mutually reinforcing rights."

29 *Ibid.*, par. 32: "In any case, the EU will recall, when appropriate, that the right to freedom of religion or belief, as enshrined in relevant international standards, does not include the right to have a religion or a belief that is free from criticism or ridicule."

30 In the guidelines there is an explicit reference to the need to intervene in such scenario: "Recall at all appropriate occasions that laws that criminalize blasphemy restrict expression concerning religious or other beliefs; that they are often applied so as to persecute, mistreat, or intimidate persons belonging to religious or other minorities, and that they can have a serious inhibiting effect on freedom of expression and on freedom of religion or belief; and recommend the decriminalization of such offences." *Ibid.*, par. 32 b).

31 At par. 34 b) it is specified that the European Union: "[...] will call on states to promote, through the educational system and other means, respect for diversity and mutual understanding by encouraging a wider knowledge of the diversity of religions and beliefs within their jurisdiction." Ibid., par. 34 b).

32 A specific goal of this initiative is to support: "[...] international, state and non-state actors in their efforts to educate the broader population on international legal standards and on the destructive effects of discrimination on its victims and on the well-being of society at large," par. 37 d).

The fifth priority action area concerns the sensitive area of religious conversion.[33] In this case, a specific commitment to European diplomacy is required, so that all necessary actions may be taken to support the abrogation of laws that punish conversion or apostasy, particularly in cases where the penalty is imprisonment or the death penalty.[34]

The sixth priority action area concerns the protection of the manifestation of religious freedom. First, it emphasizes the exceptional nature of allowable limitations of this right.[35] In this case, the EU's action will be focused on ensuring that the determination of limitations applied by the states on the exercise of the right is done in a non-discriminatory manner.[36]

The seventh area of action concerns support for those who petition for the protection of human rights and religious freedom (human rights defenders). It establishes specific actions to be taken in judicial proceedings against such persons.[37]

The final priority action area concerns relations with civil society, including through the financing of initiatives for non-governmental organizations and consultations on specific initiatives.[38]

In addition to these priority areas, Section C of the Guidelines identifies the instruments available to European diplomacy. The delegations of the various states have first priority in the monitoring and early warning strategy. In fact, they are entrusted with the task of preparing the monitoring of possible violations of the right of religious freedom and identifying situations of particular criticality.[39] Questions concerning the protection of religious freedom will also be discussed during the political dialogues with non-EU countries, including through the use of ad hoc visits by EU observers.[40] Paragraph 54 identifies religious freedom as one of the priorities for the *European Instrument for Democracy and Human*

33 On this topic it is worth mentioning the report of the UN Special Rapporteur for Freedom of Religion or Belief presented to the General Assembly of the United Nations on August 13, 2012 where important distinctions are made. The report mentions: a) the right to change one's religion; b) the right to not to be obliged to convert; c) right to proselytism and to try to convince others without the exercise of coercion; d) the right of children and their parents; UN General Assembly, *Interim Report of the Special Rapporteur on Freedom of Religion or Belief*, 13/8/2021, A/67/303.

34 Council of the European Union, *EU Guidelines on the Promotion and Protection of Freedom of Religion or Belief*, par. 39. On the topic of apostasy and conversions see Paul Marshall, Nina Shea, *Silenced: How Apostasy and Blasphemy Codes Are Choking Freedom Worldwide* (Oxford: Oxford University Press, 2011).

35 According to par. 40: "Any limitation on freedom of religion or belief, including regarding places of worship and state registration of religious or belief groups, must be exceptional and in compliance with international standards." See Council of the European Union, *EU Guidelines on the Promotion and Protection of Freedom of Religion or Belief*, par. 40.

36 Very telling in this respect is par 42 e) which dictates an action of the Union: "[…] when disproportionate administrative or regulatory burden are placed on the internal affairs of religion or belief groups, and their institutions on their organisations, so as to prevent manifestation of freedom of religion or belief in community with others and in public or private and the exercise of the linked freedoms of association and peaceful assembly." *Ibid.*, par. 43 e).

37 *Ibid.*, par. 45: "EU or Member State officials will attend and observe trials of persons prosecuted for exercising their right to freedom of religion or belief. The EU or Member States officials will make every effort to visit such person in detention or prison."

38 *Ibid.*, par. 46.

39 *Ibid.*, par. 47. It is also included the evaluation of the situation of religious freedom in the periodical country reports and on the human rights country strategies and in the annual report on human rights of the European Union; see par. 48.

40 *Ibid.*, par 53.

Rights,[41] foreseeing a significant financial contribution to projects for the protection and promotion of this right. It also states that the European Union will continue its support of religious freedom within international bodies and at the United Nations.[42] It also provides for specific training for European diplomats on matters pertaining to religious freedom.[43]

The third part of the Guidelines contains instructions on the application and assessment of their impact. In addition to providing for the strengthening of cooperation and sharing of information with international bodies tasked with protecting religious freedom, it also provides for an evaluation of the operations of European diplomacy based on the Guidelines, three years after their approval.[44]

The approval of the Guidelines has also helped influence the internal dynamics of the European Parliament. In 2014, the working group on religious freedom, composed of parliamentarians from various political groups,[45] submitted its first annual report on religious freedom.[46] The report, submitted to the various commissioners of the US Commission for International Religious Freedom (attesting to the synergies and exchanges between the two sides of the Atlantic), proposes the encouragement of European institutions to give attention to religious freedom in order to stimulate more incisive action in this field.

The report uses terminology drawn from the US Commission on Religious Freedom reports.[47] In particular, similar to the US Commission, the report of the European Parliament Working Group identifies some countries as "countries of particular concern" based on three essential parameters: 1) the severity of violations of religious freedom; 2) the frequency of violations of religious freedom; 3) the type of dealings and political relations between the European Union and the country in question. As this is an informal group

41 Created in 2006, the European Instrument for Democracy and Human Rights is the most important EU instrument for the support to the activities of promotion of human rights and democracy. See Regulation (EC) No 1889/2006 of the European Parliament and of the Council of 20 December 2006 on establishing a financing instrument for the promotion of democracy and human rights worldwide and also Regulation (EU) No. 235/2014 of the European Parliament and of the Council of 11 March 2014 establishing a financing instrument for democracy and human rights worldwide which substitutes the previous regulation of 2006.

42 See Council of the European Union, *EU Guidelines on the Promotion and Protection of Freedom of Religion or Belief*, par. 59: "The EU will continue to work actively at the UN to ensure strong cross-regional support for the promotion and defence of freedom of religion or belief, the mandate and the implementation of relevant UN resolutions in that field."

43 *Ibid.*, par. 67.

44 According to par. 70 the evaluation will take place: "[…] inter alia on the basis of the reports submitted by Heads of Missions and after consultation with civil society and relevant academic experts." It is also foreseen the consultation with religious groups and non-religious organizations according to article 17 of the Lisbon Treaty. See, *ibid.*, par. 70.

45 The working group was co-chaired by Dennis De Jong and Peter Van Delen. Members of the Presidency were MEPs: Laszlo Surjan, Gianni Pittella, Pat the Cope Gallagher, Hannu Takkula and Margrete Auken. The other members were: Marian Harkin, Latima Andrikiene, Paul Rubig, Konrad Szymanski, Csaba Sogor, Nikolaos Salavrakos, Laszlo Tokes, Diane Dodds, Tomasz Poreba and Davor Ivo Stier.

46 European Parliament Working Group on Freedom of Religion of Belief, *Annual Report 2013. Conclusions and Recommendations Regarding the Situation of Freedom of Religion or Belief in the World*, available at: www.religiousfreedom.eu.

47 It is not a coincidence the fact that Knox Thames, for many years Director of Policy and Research of the U.S. Commission on International Religious Freedom has underlined the need for a closer cooperation between the United States and the European Union: "Europe and North America increasingly share a common commitment to proactively support Article 18 of the UN Declaration on Human Rights. From this convergence arises the possibility for increasing coordination at a moment when FoRB is under renewed attack." See Knox Thames, "Forging a Trans-Atlantic Partnership on Religious Freedom," p. 4.

composed of parliamentarians, the working group does not possess the resources of the US Commission on International Religious Freedom. Thus, in order to make their assessments, they make particular use of secondary sources such as the international reports of other institutions or NGOs.[48] The report identifies situations of clear violation of religious freedom, listing them according to geographical location (identifying the violating country), and by category (identifying the object of the violation). It emphasizes the importance of the role of monitoring respect for fundamental rights, which falls to the European Parliament, and that the working group proposes itself as a facilitator for the exchange of information with all international institutions tasked with protecting the right of religious freedom. In this context, the report once again emphasizes the centrality of the US Commission of International Religious Freedom.[49] Despite its non-institutional character, the European Parliament working group has succeeded, with the help of the international relationships it has been able to establish, to bring the subject of religious freedom to the attention of numerous members of the European Parliament. The working group has later been updated to the status of Intergroup with the name of "European Parliament Intergroup on Freedom of Religion or Belief and Religious Tolerance."

The 2013 report also lists some direct recommendations to European institutions. Above all, it hopes for the effective application of the Guidelines analyzed above, including through suitable training for diplomatic officials. It then sets out, based on the French model, the creation of a true *pôle religions* capable of covering the broad spectrum of topics related to religion, and not limited solely to the protection of religious freedom. Among these topics, the centrality of the role of religious groups in transitional justice and post-war reconciliation periods is emphasized.[50] Topical recommendations are followed by country-specific recommendations.

The above analysis appears to demonstrate the delineation of an initial set of EU institutions with the specific purpose of protecting and promoting the right of religious freedom

48 It is the same report that highlights this aspect: "Included were, among other sources, the EU's Annual Report on Human Rights and Democracy in the World 2012, the Pew Research Centre's various reports on this topic, the United States Commission on International Religious Freedom (USCIRF) 2013 Annual Report, the United Nations (UN) reports, the United Kingdom All Party Parliamentary Group on International Religious Freedom report and the Human Rights Without Frontiers (HRWF) World Report." See European Parliament Working Group on Freedom of Religion or Belief, ***Annual Report** 2013. Conclusions and Recommendations Regarding the Situation of Freedom of Religion or Belief in the World*, p. 4.

49 Besides the experience of the US Commission on International Religious Freedom also the initiatives from Canada are mentioned: "The EPWG on FoRB regularly sends communications to the EEAS concerning individual cases, organises and participates in meetings with representatives of the EU institutions, issues press and other public statements, and engages in an intensive dialogue with civil society, including with representatives of religious and belief organizations. The EPWG has condemned various instances of religious violence, such as the September 2013 bombing of the All Saints Church in Peshawar, Pakistan. The EPWG also maintains regular contacts with the US Commission on International Religious Freedom and the Ambassador on international religious freedom of the United States and Canada," *ibid.*, p. 16.

50 As it is possible to read in the report: "We therefore strongly recommend that the EEAS engages in a permanent dialogue with organizations such as the World Conference of Religions for Peace. This international NGO established national and regional inter-religious councils as well as a world council. It brings together religious leaders from many different regions and has a long-standing experience with conflict resolution and reconciliation efforts." European Parliament Working Group on Freedom of Religion or Belief, *Annual Report 2013. Conclusions and Recommendations Regarding the Situation of Freedom of Religion or Belief in the World*, p. 17.

in the external relations of the EU. Despite the influence of the United States, we are still far from the creation of structures comparable to those in Washington. In the future, however, as Knox Thames hypothesized, there could be increasingly closer collaboration with the U.S. Commission on International Religious Freedom and other US institutions tasked with the protection and promotion of religious freedom.[51]

5. Religious freedom and asylum

The promotion and protection of the right of religious freedom are of increasing interest to European institutions due to the significant migratory flows caused by constitutional transitions in several countries on the Mediterranean, and the rise of fundamentalist movements such as the "Islamic State" in Syria and Iraq.[52] Indeed, a rising number of people, fleeing political persecution due to their religious faith, are requesting asylum in various European countries, which now must face new political and legal problems, both with regard to accepting asylum requesters and the assigning of refugee status.[53]

The significance of the governance of the right of asylum, in the context of policies of protection and promotion of the right of religious freedom, clearly emerged in the United States with the approval of the International Religious Freedom Act. In fact, as can be seen in US regulations, reports on the violation of religious freedom are a primary source for evaluating the existence of persecution in their countries of origin, and the possible granting of asylum by the judges tasked to rule on such requests.[54]

Section 602 of the International Religious Freedom Act devotes particular attention to the topic, establishing that the annual State Department report must be considered an important source in evaluating requests for asylum,[55] and requiring special training for

51 Knox Thames does a good survey of these initiatives; see Knox Thames, "Forging a Trans-Atlantic Partnership on Religious Freedom." Thames urges for a further development of multilateral initiatives: "The challenges of the 21st century –growing violent religious extremism, repressive majoritarian impulses, and a return to authoritarianism – call for a new approach. To be sure, traditional bilateral engagements with countries of concern are needed and should be increased. But they can be more effective and impactful if pursued in concert with others." *Ibid.*, p.6.

52 According to the 2012 report published by the Pew Forum: "Prior to the Arab Spring, the Middle East and North Africa had the highest level of government restriction on religion and social hostilities involving religion in the world [...] government restrictions on religion in the area remained high throughout 2011, while social hostilities involving religion increased." See Katie Reilly, *Global Restrictions on Religion Increased Following the Arab Spring*, 8/7/20123, available at: www.pewresearch.org/fact-tank/2013/07/08/global-restrictions-on-religion-increased-following-the-arab-spring/.

53 On the situation in Syria see United Nations, *Report of the Independent International Commission of Inquiry on the Syrian Arab Republic. Rule of Terror: Living under ISIS in Syria*, 14/11/2014 and European Parliament, *Resolution of 18 September 2014 on the situation in Iraq and Syria, and the IS offensive, including the persecution of minorities*, 18/9/2014.

54 See Craig B. Mousin, "Standing with the Persecuted; Adjudicating Religious Asylum Claims After the Enactment of the International Religious Freedom Act," *Brigham Young University Law Review*, 2, (2003): pp. 541–592. See also U.S. Commission on International Religious Freedom, *Report on Asylum Seekers in Expedit Removal*, 8/2/2005, available at: www.uscirf.gov/reports-briefs/special-reports/report-asylum-seekers-in-expedited-removal and U.S. Commission on International Religious Freedom, *Assessing the U.S. Government's Detention of Asylum Seekers*, April 2013, available at: www.uscirf.gov/reports-briefs/special-reports/assessing-the-us-governments-detention-asylum-seekers.

55 According to sec. 601 of the International Religious Freedom Act: "The Annual Report, together with other relevant documentation, shall serve as a resource for immigration judges and consular, refugee, and asylum officers in cases involving claims of persecution on the grounds of religion. Absence of reference

officials and judges tasked with ruling on asylum requests and granting refugee status.[56] The continuous discrimination and persecution against various religious minorities, particularly Christians, have therefore contributed to the development of a European jurisprudence on the topic, highlighting how difficult it remains to follow a single approach, and how helpful reports drafted by international institutions and by those same European institutions can be in resolving various legal events, particularly for the purpose of verifying the condition of religious minorities in the countries of origin of asylum requesters.[57]

From this point of view, in some cases the reports produced by the U.S. Commission on International Religious Freedom and by the State Department have been shown to be particularly significant, often used by applicants to indicate the political situation in their country of origin with regard to the treatment of religious minorities.[58] Along with these reports, there are others produced by nongovernmental organizations such as, for example, the annual report published by the Vatican-based foundation "Aid to the Church in Need," which is specifically focused on the conditions of Christian minorities. The reliability of such reports is of fundamental importance in the general strategy for promotion and protection of religious freedom, since only if such reports are drafted with objective criteria can they be of help in evaluating the situations of applicants' countries of origins and the possible acceptance of requests for asylum.[59] For example, in a case decided by the European Human Rights Court (*Said v. The Netherlands*),[60] not directly relevant to religious freedom, but

by the Annual Report to conditions described by the alien shall not constitute the sole grounds for a denial of the alien's claim." See US Congress, *International Religious Freedom Act of 1998*.

56 According to sec. 603 b) of the International Religious Freedom Act: "The Attorney General, in consultation with the Secretary of State, the Ambassador at Large, and other relevant officials such as the Director of the National Foreign Affairs Training Centre, shall provide training to all officers adjudicating asylum cases, and to immigration officers performing duties under section 235 (b) of the Immigration and Nationality Act (8 U.S.C. 1225 (b)), on the nature of religious persecutions abroad, including country-specific conditions, instruction on methods of religious persecution practiced in foreign countries, and applicable distinctions within a country in the treatment of various religious practice and believers." Section 603 c) mandates a specific training for judges: "The Executive Office of Immigration Review of the Department of Justice shall incorporate into its initial and ongoing training of immigration judges training on the extent and nature of religious persecution internationally, including country-specific conditions, and including use of the Annual Report. Such training shall include governmental and non-governmental methods of persecution employed, and differences in the treatment of religious groups by such persecuting entities." *Ibid*.

57 For a detailed analysis of the case law of European supranational courts see Pasquale Annicchino, "The Persecution of Religious and LGBTI Minorities and Asylum Law: Recent Trends in the Adjudication of European Supranational Courts," *European Public Law* 21, no. 3, 2015, pp. 571–590.

58 In deciding the case *F.H. v. Sweden*, concerning an Iraqi national of Christian faith which has submitted an asylum request in Sweden fearing possible religious persecutions, the European Court of Human Rights did not take into account the observations made by minority judges which in their dissenting opinion made explicit reference to many international reports where the situation of Christians in Iraq was defined as precarious. *See*, ECtHR, *F.H. v. Sweden* (32621/06) 20/1/2009, dissenting opinion of Judges Power-Forde and Zupančič.

59 According to Pasquale Ferrara: "In terms of policy consequences, it seems that reports originating from governmental monitoring activities are more effective. However, such a result comes at the expenses of legitimacy; one may argue that there is a clear trade-off between the wide acceptance of a report on religious freedom and the limited supranational powers of the international institution concerned than to the 'credibility' of the report itself. In a way, 'national' or intergovernmental reports are 'documents with teeth', whereas international reports are 'documents with trust'." Pasquale Ferrara, "Reporting on religious freedom: the 'governmental' approach and the issue of legitimacy," in Pasquale Annicchino, *Freedom of Religion or Belief in Foreign Policy. Which one?*, p. 61.

60 European Court of Human Rights, *Said v. The Netherlands*, (2345/02), 5/7/2005.

nevertheless relevant for purposes of our analysis, a judge criticized the reports on human rights published by the State Department, as they were not considered a "credible source" for purposes of verifying the status of the protection of human rights in the world.[61] The production of the initial European reports on the subject, are then shown to be of fundamental importance, since recently the Court of Justice of the European Union also was called to decide in the case *Y and Z v. Germany*,[62] which involved persecutions against religious minorities.

Developments in the European Union related to the protection and promotion of religious freedom indicate a constant and growing interest within Brussels institutions. This is true both with regard to regulations approved, which we have seen in the Guidelines, and cases that the Luxembourg judges (and those in Strasbourg, with regard to the European Council) are called upon to decide. Decisions related to requests for asylum due to religious persecution further highlight the significance for the EU countries of the protection of religious freedom in non-EU countries. Thus, some of them have created institutions specifically tasked with promoting and protecting this right. This has been the case for Italy, France, and the United Kingdom, among others, as we will see.

61 In his opinion judge Loucaides agrees with the majority but criticizes the use of reports such as the one published by the US Department of State: "I cannot agree with the inclusion in the judgment (par. 35) of the U.S. Department of State Country Report on Human Rights Practices in Eritrea as a reliable source of information on the human rights situation in the country. This is because I do not consider such reports to be credible sources of information on human rights in any part of the world. They are not prepared by an independent and impartial institution but by a purely political government agency, which promotes and expresses the foreign policy of the United States. Therefore, they cannot by definition be relied on as a neutral and impartial exposition of the facts mentioned therein. There is always an element of suspicion that such reports are influenced by political expediency based on U.S. foreign policy with reference to the situation in the country concerned and that they serve a political agenda. Therefore, I do not see how any judgment of the European Court of Human Rights can rely in any way or to any extent on any U.S. Department of State Country Report on Human Rights Practices in respect of any country." *Ibid.*, dissenting opinion judge Loucaides.

62 Court of Justice of the European Union, *Y and Z v. Germany*. For a comment on the decision see Julian M. Lehmann, "Persecution, Concealment and the Limits of a Human Rights Approach in (European) Asylum Law. The Case of Germany v. Y and Z in the Court of Justice of the European Union," *International Journal of Refugee Law*, 26, no. 1, (2014): pp. 65–81.

References

McCrea, Ronan, *Religion and the Public Order of the European Union* (Oxford: Oxford University Press, 2010).

Annicchino, Pasquale, "The Persecution of Religious and LGBTI Minorities and Asylum Law: Recent Trends in the Adjudication of European Supranational Courts," *European Public Law* 21, no. 3, 2015, pp. 571–590.

Annicchino, Pasquale, "Freedom of Religion or Belief in the Foreign Policy of the European Union. Much Ado About Nothing?" in Mary A. Glendon, and R. Alvira (eds.), *Religion and Civil Society: The Changing Faces of Religion and Secularity* (New York: Georg Olms, 2014), pp. 115–129.

Annicchino, Pasquale, "The New Guidelines on Freedom of Religion and LGBTI Rights in the External Action of the European Union," *European Human Rights Law Review*, 6, (2013): pp. 624–630.

Catholic News Agency, "Full Text of Pope Francis interview with 'La Vanguardia,'" 13/6/2014, available at: www.catholicnewsagency.com/news/pope-francis-interview-with-la-vanguardia---full-text-45430/.

COMECE, *Religious Freedom. Pillar of the Human Rights Policy in the External Relations* (Brussels: Comece, 2010).

De Jong, Dennis, "The Role of the European Parliament in Helping to Protect Freedom of Religion or Belief via the EU's External Relations," in Pasquale Annicchino (eds.), *Freedom of Religion or Belief in Foreign Policy. Which one?* (Florence: EUI University Press, 2013), pp. 43–47.

European Parliament Working Group on Freedom of Religion of Belief, *Annual Report 2013. Conclusions and Recommendations Regarding the Situation of Freedom of Religion or Belief in the World*, available at: www.religiousfreedom.eu.

European Platform for Secularism in Europe, "EU to Defend Freedom of Religion and Secular Democracy in External Policies," 7/11/2011, available at: http://goo-gl/rtBMS7.

Fabbri, Alberto, *Unione europea e fenomeno religioso. Alcune valutazioni di principio* (Torino: Giappichelli, 2012).

Ferrara, Pasquale, *Global Religions and International Relations. A Diplomatic Perspective* (New York: Palgrave, 2014).

Ferrara, Pasquale, "Reporting on religious freedom: the 'governmental' approach and the issue of legitimacy," in Pasquale Annicchino, *Freedom of Religion or Belief in Foreign Policy. Which one?* (EUI Press: San Domenico di Fiesole, 2013), pp. 59–65.

Lehmann, Julian M., "Persecution, Concealment and the Limits of a Human Rights Approach in (European) Asylum Law. The Case of Germany v. Y and Z in the Court of Justice of the European Union," *International Journal of Refugee Law*, 26, no. 1, (2014): pp. 65–81.

Marshall, Paul, and Shea Nina, *Silenced: How Apostasy and Blasphemy Codes Are Choking Freedom Worldwide* (Oxford: Oxford University Press, 2011).

Mousin, Craig B. "Standing with the Persecuted; Adjudicating Religious Asylum Claims After the Enactment of the International Religious Freedom Act," *Brigham Young University Law Review*, 2, (2003): pp. 541–592.

Reilly, Katie, *Global Restrictions on Religion Increased Following the Arab Spring*, 8/7/20123, available at: www.pewresearch.org/fact-tank/2013/07/08/global-restrictions-on-religion-increased-following-the-arab-spring/.

Thames, Knox, "Forging a Trans-Atlantic Partnership on Religious Freedom," *The Review of Faith and International Affairs* 12, no. 3, (2014): pp. 1–8.

UN General Assembly, *Interim Report of the Special Rapporteur on Freedom of Religion or Belief*, 13/8/2021, A/67/303

United Nations, *Report of the Independent International Commission of Inquiry on the Syrian Arab Republic. Rule of Terror: Living under ISIS in Syria*, 14/11/2014 and European Parliament,

Resolution of 18 September 2014 on the situation in Iraq and Syria, and the IS offensive, including the persecution of minorities, 18/9/2014.

US Commission on International Religious Freedom, *Report on Asylum Seekers in Expedit Removal*, 8/2/2005, available at: www.uscirf.gov/reports-briefs/special-reports/report-asylum-seekers-in-expedited-removal

US Commission on International Religious Freedom, *Assessing the U.S. Government's Detention of Asylum Seekers*, April 2013, available at: www.uscirf.gov/reports-briefs/special-reports/assessing-the-us-governments-detention-asylum-seekers.

6 Reception of the United States model in the experiences of several European countries

1. Italy

The model developed in the United States with the approval of the International Religious Freedom Act has had significant influence, inspiring the legislation of various European countries. As we have seen above, it has certainly been a reference point for EU initiatives, but it has also had an impact in regard to some specifically national initiatives. For example, in the last several years in Italy, through the action of the Ministry of Foreign Affairs, interest has grown in the promotion and protection of religious freedom, although the fragmentary nature of the political system and the continuous alternation of new ministers has not facilitated the development of a unified or coherent action.[1] The origin of the interest of the Italian Ministry of Foreign Affairs in religion in general is not recent, although, as Pasquale Ferrara points out, the subject of religious freedom has never been explicitly articulated.[2]

Franco Frattini was probably the first Foreign Minister to address the topic and to make it a possible priority of Italian foreign policy. He had attempted to do this in his previous role as a European Commissioner. As Frattini pointed out:

> Before my arrival at the Ministry of Foreign Affairs, only partial attention was paid to religious freedom, in the sense that this topic was not included as a true resource and priority for Italian foreign policy. In my first term, I did not give priority attention to this right, though I did so in my second term, thanks to my experience in Europe during my time as Vice President of the Commission.[3]

1 For an introduction to the topic see Pasquale Annicchino, "La tutela e la promozione del diritto di libertà religiosa nelle recenti iniziative di politica estera italiana," *Quaderni di Diritto e Politica Ecclesiastica*, 1, (2014): pp. 51–66 and Pasquale Annicchino, "Recent Developments Concerning the Promotion of Freedom of Religion or Belief in Italian Foreign Policy," *The Review of Faith and International Affairs* 11, no. 3, (2013): pp. 61–68.

2 As Pasquale Ferrara argues: "Traditionally the Italian foreign policy after World War II, during the Christian-Democrat led governments, has not articulated in an explicit manner the issue of religious freedom as a leading topic of international relations. This does not mean, however, that Italian foreign policy ignored the issue; rather, religious freedom was 'embedded' in the Italian approach to North Africa and the Middle East, as one of the many aspects of the Italian 'projection' in the Mediterranean." See Pasquale Ferrara, "Reporting on religious freedom: the 'governmental' approach and the issue of legitimacy," in Pasquale Annicchino (ed.), *Protecting and Promoting Freedom of Religion or Belief in Foreign Policy. Which One?*, p. 61.

3 Interview to Franco Frattini, Minister for Foreign Affairs of the second Berlusconi Government (2002–2004); European Commissioner for Justice, Freedom and Security (2004–2008); Minister for Foreign

The need for a study of matters related to the right of religious freedom was quite obvious to Franco Frattini as early as 2006, when the European Union Agency for Fundamental Rights was instituted, such that Frattini himself requested more incisive action on the topic.[4] In effect, as Frattini says, at first the Agency included in its operational mandate action on anti-Semitism, Christianophobia, and Islamophobia.[5] But in later years, the Agency did not focus its attention on religious freedom, prioritizing other matters instead, and for this reason as well, after his appointment as Minister in the fourth Berlusconi government, Franco Frattini attempted to bring the topic to the attention of the Italian Ministry of Foreign Affairs through the creation of an interministerial task force. The development of an Italian action, however, is not due to the initiative of Franco Frattini alone. As we have previously seen in the US context, the establishment of specialized institutions with the specific mandate of promoting and protecting religious freedom is often influenced by religious actors, who are usually on the front lines in an international context where persecutions against religious minorities are being committed. On the one hand, we must admit that broad sectors of the government and the political majority of the fourth Berlusconi government repeatedly emphasized the significance of religion, particularly as an identity, in their political agenda; on the other hand, with regard to specific action on religious freedom, there has been particular interest, as Franco Frattini himself has said, by the Holy See, which has maintained an open and continuous dialogue with the Ministry of Foreign Affairs.[6]

The action initiated by Franco Frattini was then continued in subsequent years with the appointment of Giulio Terzi di Sant'Agata to the Ministry of Foreign Affairs on November 16, 2011. Like his predecessor, Terzi di Sant'Agata's actions were based on a continuous dialogue with the Holy See. As Terzi di Sant'Agata said:

> [...] the collaboration with the Holy See is fundamental for diplomatic action to defend the rights of persons against attacks by those we can call the new barbarians, that is,

Affairs of the fourth Berlusconi Government (2008–2011) quoted in Pasquale Annicchino, "La tutela e la promozione del diritto di libertà religiosa nelle recenti iniziative di politica estera italiana," p. 54.

4 As Frattini argues: "The experience in Brussels was very important for me also because as Commissioner for Justice and Security human rights were within my competence. It is for this reason that I worked to create the European Union Agency for Fundamental Rights as I taught that religious freedom, non-discrimination and women rights should have been the rights on which to base a European action in this field." *Ibid.*

5 Franco Frattini is skeptical of the action of the European Union Agency for Fundamental Rights on religious freedom after 2006: "At the beginning the Agency should have worked on three topics: antisemitism, christianofobia and islamofobia meaning the extent to which there are discriminations against the believers of the three most important monotheistic religions. This is what I asked in 2006. I left in January 2008 and since then the agency has focused on topics different from religious freedom." *Ibid.*

6 On the role and position of the Holy See on the international protection of religious freedom see Tarcisio Bertone, "La Diplomazia Pontificia e la Libertà Religiosa," in Mary A. Glendon, Hans F. Zacher (ed.), *Universal Rights in a World of Diversity. The Case of Religious Freedom* (Vatican City: Pontifical Academy of Social Sciences, 2012): pp. 607–618. The interest of the Holy See in the action of the Italian Minister for Foreign Affairs is confirmed also by Franco Frattini which acknowledges how concrete actions, such as the building of houses for Christians in Iraq, were born out of the cooperation between the two institutions: "I have had a very good relationship with the Holy See, and especially with Cardinal Tauran, with Monsignor Mamberti and also with the Secretary of State Cardianl Bertone and with President Bagnasco. I have had several meetings with them and we have cooperated for instance on the issue of persecution against Christians in the Middle East. Another concrete initiative has been the construction of houses for couples of young Arab Christians in Iraq in the province of Ninive and in Jerusalem. We have helped them

those who deny humanity and piously invoke God, scorn dialogue, and revile peaceful coexistence.[7]

Through a two-year memorandum of understanding signed with the city of Rome (not renewed by the subsequent Minister),[8] Minister Terzi di Sant'Agata also attempted to institute the Religious Freedom Monitoring Center, intending to "undertake a joint path of study, analysis, and monitoring of conditions regarding religious freedom, with specific reference to the socio-cultural context of Rome."[9] The memorandum set out the minimum organizational parameters for the Monitoring Center, leaving broad room for discretion, referring to Article 3, paragraph three of internal regulations, and was therefore a particularly agile regulatory text, omitting precise instructions for the actual operational methods of the institution. The project initiated by Minister Terzi Sant'Agata to establish the Monitoring Center, as previously noted, was subsequently terminated, since the succeeding government, headed by Mario Monti,[10] did not renew the memorandum of understanding between the Ministry of Foreign Affairs and the City of Rome. The Monitoring Center must therefore be considered defunct.[11] However, at the Ministry of

because they didn't want to leave from there." Quoted in Pasquale Annicchino, "La tutela e la promozione del diritto di libertà religiosa nelle recenti iniziative di politica estera italiana," p. 55.

7 *Ibid.*, p. 59. Also Giulio Terzi di Sant'Agata has underlined the central role of the right to freedom of religion within the context of his own political action. See Giulio Terzi di Sant'Agata, "Una forte azione politica e diplomatica a tutela della libertà religiosa," *L'Osservatore Romano*, 19/6/2012 and also Minister of Foreign Affairs, "Attacchi e violenze contro i cristiani-Terzi all'UE, applicare piano libertà religiosa," 27/11/2011, available at: www.esteri.it/mae/it/sala_stampa/archivionotizie/approfondimenti/2011/12/20111227_terziue.html. During a public speech at the annual Meeting of Comunione e Liberazione Terzi di Sant'Agata has also underlined the influence of Italian actions in this field: "We must recognized that the topic of religion has been excluded for too much time by analysts of international politics [...] During the course of the last nine month Italy has brought it back to the center of the international debate also by stressing the importance of the right to religious freedom. In every institutional meeting, on every occasion I met with the leaders of the countries of the Arab Spring I have underlined how, for Italy, it is fundamental to protect religious freedom and minorities' rights [...] We have insisted in Brussels to push forward this agenda also within the external action of the European Union. We also suggested to create a European task force asking to the High Representative to report periodically on the status of religious freedom in the world. Finally, we have also endorsed the approval of EU Guidelines on freedom of religion or belief." Giulio Terzi di Sant'Agata, *Intervento al Meeting Rimini 2012, Politica Internationale e Libertà Religiosa*, 24/8/2012, available at: www.meetingrimini.org/default.asp?id=673&item=5513.

8 Protocollo d'intesa fra Roma Capitale e il Ministero degli Affari Esteri signed in Rome on 10 January, 2012. The Ministry in commenting this memorandum makes explicit reference to the American experience: "After United States, Canada and other countries also Italy has now a monitoring institution aimed at fighting violation of religious freedom in the world starting from the countries where minorities are persecuted." Ministry of Foreign Affairs, "Roma: anche in Italia un osservatorio sulla libertà religiosa," 22/6/2012, available at: www.esteri.it/mae/it/sala_stampa/archivionotizie/approfondimenti/2012/06/20120622_roma.html.

9 Protocollo d'intesa fra Roma Capitale e il Ministero degli Affari Esteri, art. 2.

10 Mario Monti has been Prime Minister from 16/11/2011 to 27/4/2013. Giulio Terzi di Sant'Agata has been Minister for Foreign Affairs from 16/11/2011 to 26/3/2013.

11 According to Knox Thames, this was however an experience worth mentioning in the context of global actions on religious freedom: "Italy, for two years, established a special observatory on freedom of religion, a hybrid partnership between the Ministry of Foreign Affairs and the mayor of Rome. However, its actions were minimal and the next government allowed it to close by not renewing its mandate." Knox Thames, *Forging a Trans-Atlantic Partnership on Religious Freedom*, p. 2.

Foreign Affairs, attention to religious freedom seems to be present, particularly through the influence of the Italian government in the process that led to the approval of the European Guidelines of June 2013,[12] and also with regard to certain events such as the one that led to the release of Meriam Ibrahim, a Christian convert sentenced to death in Sudan for apostasy.[13] Indeed, Meriam was released as a result of the pressure exercised by the Italian Ministry of Foreign Affairs, in concert with other governments.[14]

2. France

The French experience is different from those previously analyzed (the US, the EU, and Italy, and the British and Canadian experiences, which will be discussed later), since the institutions and procedures created at the French Ministry of Foreign Affairs do not directly address the promotion and protection of religious freedom, but relations with religious communities in other countries, particularly in areas where there are political tensions motivated by religion. The object of the French initiatives seems to be the "geo-politics of religion," wherein a specific role is assigned to the right of religious freedom.[15] It therefore seems worthy of note, particularly for a better understanding of the European scene.

The 2008 White Paper on National Security had previously emphasized the importance of religion in understanding geopolitical phenomena and international politics, and just one year later in 2009, Bernard Kouchner, appointed Minister of Foreign Affairs, ordered

[12] The role of the Italian influence is acknowledged by Franco Frattini: "The European model was born out of the constant relationship we had developed within the context of Italian foreign policy. At the European level there was a complex negotiation because initially my proposal was rejected, mainly because the protection was exclusively focused on Christians. This was soon solved. Some countries had doubts on whether the EU could not only affirm this principle but also intervene within the internal affairs of other countries. A compromise prevailed by enacting a first phase based on monitoring and reports. This, according to my understanding, had to be only the first phase but runs the risk of remaining the only one," quoted in Pasquale Annicchino, *La tutela e la promozione del diritto di libertà religiosa nelle recenti iniziative di politica estera italiana*, p. 57.

[13] On this case see Amnesty International, "Sudan: Woman Facing Death Sentence on Grounds of her Religion Must be Released," 14/5/2014, available at: www.amnestyusa.org/news/news-item/sudan-woman-facing-death-sentence-on-grounds-of-her-religion-must-be-released, and also Pasquale Annicchino, 'A Transatlantic Partnership on International Religious Freedom? The United States, Europe and the Challenge of Religious Persecution, *Oxford Journal of Law and Religion* 5, no. 2, 2016: pp. 280–297.

[14] On July 17, 2014 the European Parliament approved a resolution on this case – see European Parliament, *European Parliament Resolution of 17 July 2014 on Sudan. The case of Meriam Yahia Ibrahim (2014/2727 (RSP))*. The text of the resolution makes explicit reference to the EU guidelines on freedom of religion or belief and to the clauses part of the Cotonou commercial agreements ratified also by Sudan. The resolutions stresses how religious freedom is: "[…] a universal human right that needs to be protected everywhere and for everyone; whereas Sudan has ratified the UN and African Union conventions and thus has an International obligation to defend and promote freedom of religion or belief, which includes the right to adopt, change or abandon one's religion or belief of one's own free will." See point (G) of the resolution.

[15] See the intervention by Jospeh Maïla, former director of the pôle religions of the Minister of Foreign Affairs, at the "Forum du futur" titled *Géopolitique des religions*, 15/4/2000, available at: www.france-ameriques.org/150410.pdf.

the creation of a *pôle religions*, appointing Joseph Maïla as director.[16] The *pôle religions* promoted by Bernard Kouchner was intended to pursue three major goals:

- observation and analysis of the role and influence of religion and religious groups on the global scene[17];
- collection and categorization of information[18];
- training of French diplomats on matters regarding the political aspect of religious phenomena.

The birth of French interest in the establishment of a *pôle religions* was explained by Joseph Maïla during a hearing held before the French parliament in 2010. According to Maïla, the fall of the Berlin Wall and the consequent crisis of the communist regime triggered a different search for meaning and identity, which previously had culminated in political ideologies, and which now instead was often filled by the bonding power of religious identity.[19] One example that could help to clarify the process now underway in many parts of the world, according to Maïla, is in the former Yugoslavia where, once the single-state identity had fallen away, religious identities, with all their problems, rose up and helped unleash further conflicts.[20]

With specific regard to religious freedom, Joseph Maïla notes some criticisms by the U.S. State Department of certain French policies regarding, for example, the treatment of certain religious movements such as Scientology.[21] In sum, according to Joseph Maïla, the subject

16 As Christian Bernard underlines, the structures is not particularly complex and has few resources: "This unit was created under the direction of Joseph Maïla that, at the same time, became director of the 'Prospective' (a direction which includes the pôle religions). There are few resources and it is a little structure, Joseph Maïla has only two assistants. Notwithstanding these limitations they do a remarkable job. Joseph Maïla, of Lebanese origins, scholar and specialist of the Middle East, of Islam and sociology of conflict has been rector of the Institut Catholique of Paris, and director of the Research Centre on Peace and of the Institute on Mediation and Negotiation." See Christian Bernard, "La République laïque et la religion: une nouveauté, un pôle Religions," 4/1/2011, available at: www.institut-jacquescartier.fr/tags/pole-religions/.

17 According to Christian Bernard: "The pôle religions studies all the evolutions, tensions that affect all religions, in particular (but not only) Islam. It also focuses on the evangelical churches, the evolution of orthodox churches especially in Russia where nationalism and religion appear to be particularly connected (teaching on religion is now mandatory in the schools of 16 provinces out of 26). The unit also focuses on Buddhism especially in Thailand and Birmania." *Ibid.*

18 According to Christian Bernard: "The pôle religions is able to produce reports on the role of religion in the different countries of the world. This is a real pragmatic function. Sometimes these data are useful in situation of crisis but it can also be useful in another fashion." *Ibid.*

19 As J. Maïla has argued: "First of all, after the fall of the Berlin wall and the end of ideological mobilizations which had polarized the world for fifty years, the offer of 'meaning' has been reducing leaving more space to different beliefs. After the globalization and the process of anonymization linked to it we have seen a return of the different identities. This is what Freud called "the narcissism of little differences" which is possible to explain through the context of standardization of life and behaviours." See Assemblée Nationale, *Compte rendu Commission des affaires étrangèrs*, 13/1/2010, p. 1.

20 This example is understood to be of fundamental importance also by Joseph Maïla during his hearing before the Assemblée Nationale: "[...] in certain pluri-communitarian communities where religion has always played a role the crisis of the State and the social fragmentation pushes the different groups to invoke a religious identity as a substitute of politics. For example, since when Jugoslavian citizenship did not signify anything the Bosnian, Serbian and Croatian communities they all started to reshape their own identity on the bases of religion." *Ibid.*, p. 3.

21 In his intervention Joseph Maïla makes many references to issues discussed within the context of the United Nations: "French diplomacy is now more often asked to intervene on certain issues. The issue

of the role of religious groups and religious freedom was made central to international relations in the context of the global protection of human rights. This point of observation is particularly important for France which, influenced by the paradigm of *laïcité* in its interpretation of international relations, has often ruled out an interpretation of international dynamics that duly considers the role of religion. However, the establishment of *pôle religions* appears to belie this paradigm.

With regard to the topic of promotion and protection of religious freedom, Joseph Maïla further emphasizes two aspects: on the one hand, the difficulties encountered by the universalism of Western human rights in an increasingly pluralized world, and on the other the precarious situation of Christians in the Middle East which, as we have seen, is a constant of many initiatives regarding the promotion of religious freedom:

> In addition to the radicalization taking place in Iraq or Egypt, we must note the demographic disintegration and weakening of Christian communities. Because of the war, the number of Christians in Iraq has gone from 1.2 million to 500,000 or 600,000. The Christian populations in Palestine or Lebanon are also experiencing an erosion.[22]

Joseph Maïla's narrative accurately reflects the positions of French diplomacy, which seems to show notable interest in the role of religion in international policy. The French position, as we have seen, is specifically characterized by its interest in religious communities, including from a national security perspective,[23] with the right of religious freedom taking only second place. However, it remains an approach to be duly considered, especially given the French influence in the external relations of the European Union.

3. The United Kingdom

The United Kingdom is also one of the countries that have included the protection and promotion of religious freedom as one of its foreign policy objectives. Baroness Sayeeda Warsi, appointed Minister of State for Faith and Communities under the David Cameron

related to the cartoons of the prophet Mohammad has been particularly challenging for many countries and also for us. Under the name 'contemporary form of racism' a real battle has been fought at the UN Human Rights Council on the issue of defamation of religions and blasphemy. Certain states, members of the Organization for the Islamic Conference, wanted to introduce the possibility to criminalize the defamation of religions. On the other side our American allies stress very much the role of freedom of religion in their yearly reports and France is also often criticized for instance on the treatment of scientologists or on the issue of the Muslim veil." *Ibid*., pp. 4–5.

22 *Ibid*., p. 11.

23 Within the French context it is also important to underline the role of the Minister of Defence which has been constantly following the evolution of the debate on the relationships between national security and religion. This has been underlined by Eric German which works at the Ministry as an advisor on strategic affairs: "We do not have any doctrine of Religious Engagement (RE) per se. But in various theaters of operation where French troops are deployed, they have a regular and fruitful dialogue with local religious leaders, grassroots communities, and faith-based NGOs [...] We surely have to take religion much more seriously and this is true at the European and at a NATO level." See Judd Birdsall, "Eric Germain on French Foreign Policy and Religion," *The Review of Faith and International Affairs* 12, no. 3, (2014): pp. 73–74. It is also worth mentioning the work done by Pharos – an organization engaged since 2009 in monitoring cultural and religious pluralism in many countries of the world. See www.observatoirepharos.com.

government,[24] has stressed that the question of religious freedom has now become a global priority, and therefore a matter of fundamental importance for the UK government.[25] To this end, according to Sayeeda Warsi, the strategy to adopt should be an international partnership with the governments of countries that have demonstrated sensitivity toward the topic.[26] The British government should therefore aspire to be a spokesperson for persecuted religious minorities.

In March 2014, the Foreign Office Group on Freedom of Religion or Belief was officially established as a sub-group of the Human Rights Advisory Group.[27] Previously, the Foreign Office has produced some guidelines to orient the activities of diplomatic personnel and support the protection and promotion of religious freedom. The text, entitled *Freedom of Religion or Belief: How the FCO Can Help Promote Respect for this Human Right*,[28] would become one of the sources of inspiration for the guidelines subsequently approved by the European Council and made available to the European External Action Service. The text, though not legally binding, provides important instruction on how officials of the Foreign and Commonwealth Office[29] should conceptualize the right of religious freedom and relate to it, and defines a broad notion of religious freedom that includes not only the major religious denominations, but also "convictions" such as veganism.[30]

The efforts of the United Kingdom were not limited only to the action of the Foreign and Commonwealth Office, but were then extended with the creation of a parliamentary intergroup called the All Party Parliamentary Group on Freedom of Religion or Belief,[31]

24 Sayeeda Warsi was appointed as a Minister on September 4, 2012 and resigned on August 5, 2014. She resigned because she did not share the position of the British government on the conflict between Israel and Palestine after the events of July 2014.

25 The important role played by Baroness Warsi is underlined by Sue Breeze which served as head of a team responsible for the UK's work to promote and protect freedom of religion within the Human Rights and Democracy Department of the Foreign and Commonwealth Office. See Judd Birdsall, "Sue Breeze on British Foreign Policy and Religion," *The Review of Faith and International Affairs* 12, no. 3, (2014): pp. 37–41.

26 According to Sayeeda Warsi: "The UK government is fighting against religious persecutions and this action needs an international consensus. To this extent the last September in New York I have organized a meeting with international political leaders to explore the different possibilities to act to protect and promote freedom of religion or belief and to fight religious intolerance in our societies," see Sayeeda Warsi, "Le minacce alla libertà religiosa. Una crisi divenuta globale," *L'Osservatore Romano*, 11/1/2014.

27 As underlined by Sue Breeze: "I anticipate that they will be influential in shaping the direction of our work. We may well work with the Advisory Group on ramping up our work in a new set of priorities countries." See Judd Birdsall, "Sue Breeze on British Foreign Policy and Religion," p. 76.

28 Foreign and Commonwealth Office, *Freedom of Religion or Belief. How the FCO Can Help Promote Respect for this Human Right*, 20/10/2016, available at: www.gov.uk/government/publications/freedom-of-religion-or-belief-how-the-fco-can-help-promote-respect-for-this-human-right.

29 The text has been used also in the training of diplomats. As Sue Breeze underlines: "In some cases there is a nervousness about how to deal with faith communities. We have tried to dispel some of these worries by developing a toolkit that is designed to help Foreign and Commonwealth Office (FCO) staff in our Embassies and High Commissions across the world understand what exactly the right to FoRB covers and give them some tools for promoting it. We also provide training for staff on religious literacy – both through a one-day training course and a regular series of lunchtime seminars." See Judd Birdsall, "Sue Breeze on British Foreign Policy and Religion," p. 76.

30 Foreign and Commonwealth Office, *Freedom of Religion or Belief. How the FCO Can Help Promote Respect for this Human Right*, p. 4.

31 The goals of the intergroup are defined in the following terms: "To raise awareness and profile of International religious freedom as a human right among parliamentarians, media, government and the

presided over by Baroness Elizabeth Berridge and including parliamentarians from all political parties. The group receives support, including economic support, from various religious communities. The group's objective is to sensitize the government on the topic of protection of religious freedom in an international context. For this purpose, an initial report was produced, entitled *Article 18: An Orphaned Right*, which lists numerous cases of violation of the right of religious freedom. The introduction to the report made it clear that the initiative of the United Kingdom took into account the debate already in progress in other countries on the numerous cases of persecution and discrimination against religious minorities[32]:

> The group received evidence of persecution and discrimination from across the religion and belief spectrum, but notes that a particularly heavy price is being paid by Christians. As vice-chair of the group, Baroness Cox, outlined in a recent House of Lords debate: "The faith tradition now suffering the most widespread and systematic violations of religious freedom is Christianity. It is estimated that there are at least 250m Christians suffering persecution today, from harassment, intimidation and imprisonment to torture and execution." However, as the evidence demonstrates, persecution is determinedly not confined to any particular tradition, but common to all the major faiths, as well as many newer and less well-known beliefs, and those people who eschew religion entirely.[33]

The report also responds to the choices of the Foreign and Commonwealth Office, which in its 2012 Human Rights report identified the right of religious freedom as one of the priorities for its action. The example of the United Kingdom also demonstrates the attempt at convergence underway among several Western countries, starting with US initiatives, to make the protection and promotion of the right of religious freedom a renewed priority on the international scene. However, this convergence is not a foregone conclusion. Indeed, it is increasingly called into question by initiatives that tend to challenge a notion of religious freedom associated with the initiatives of Western countries, perceived as overly attentive to the individual dimension and less to the institutional and collective aspects. As we will see, these initiatives are often the result of a rethinking of the notion of religious freedom, coming from religious groups themselves.[34]

general public in the UK; and to increase effectiveness and awareness of the UK's contribution to international institutions charged with enforcing this human right." See http://anorphanedright.net/about. See also Baroness Berridge of the Vale of Catmose, "The All Party Parliamentary Group on International Freedom of Religion or Belief," *Ecclesiastical Law Journal* 17, 1, (2015): pp. 36–41.

32 Sue Breeze underlines the strong cooperation with US and Canadian institutions: "We worked closely with our US colleagues and benefited from their advice on the development of our training course, and it has been good to be able to share our experience in training with our Canadian colleagues. We can only benefit from working more closely together." See Judd Birdsall, "Sue Breeze on British Foreign Policy and Religion," p. 76.

33 All Parliamentary Group on Freedom of Religion or Belief, *Article 18: An Orphaned Right*, available at: www.religiousfreedom.eu/wp-content/uploads/2015/07/World-2013-2.pdf, 2013, p. 2.

34 For an introduction to the topic see Jeffrey Haynes, *Faith-based Organisations and the United Nations*, ReligioWest working paper, RSCAS 2013/70, 2013.

References

All Parliamentary Group on Freedom of Religion or Belief, *Article 18: An Orphaned Right*, 2013, available at: www.religiousfreedom.eu/wp-content/uploads/2015/07/World-2013-2.pdf.

Amnesty International, "Sudan: Woman Facing Death Sentence on Grounds of her Religion Must be Released," 14/5/2014, available at: www.amnestyusa.org/news/news-item/sudan-woman-facing-death-sentence-on-grounds-of-her-religion-must-be-released.

Annicchino, Pasquale, "A Transatlantic Partnership on International Religious Freedom? The United States, Europe and the Challenge of Religious Persecution," *Oxford Journal of Law and Religion* 5, no. 2, 2016: pp. 280–297.

Annicchino, Pasquale, "La tutela e la promozione del diritto di libertà religiosa nelle recenti iniziative di politica estera italiana," *Quaderni di Diritto e Politica Ecclesiastica*, 1, (2014): pp. 51–66.

Annicchino, Pasquale, "Recent Developments Concerning the Promotion of Freedom of Religion or Belief in Italian Foreign Policy," *The Review of Faith and International Affairs* 11, no. 3, (2013): pp. 61–68.

Assemblée Nationale, *Compte rendu Commission des affaires étrangèrs*, 13/1/2010.

Baroness Berridge of the Vale of Catmose, "The All Party Parliamentary Group on International Freedom of Religion or Belief," *Ecclesiastical Law Journal* 17, 1, (2015): pp. 36–41.

Bernard, Christian, "La République laïque et la religion: une nouveauté, un pôle Religions," 4/1/2011, available at: https://www.institut-jacquescartier.fr/tags/pole-religions/.

Bertone, Tarcisio, "La Diplomazia Pontificia e la Libertà Religiosa," in Mary A. Glendon, and Hans F. Zacher (ed.), *Universal Rights in a World of Diversity. The Case of Religious Freedom* (Vatican City: Pontifical Academy of Social Sciences, 2012). pp. 607–618.

Birdsall, Judd, "Eric Germain on French Foreign Policy and Religion," *The Review of Faith and International Affairs* 12, no. 3, (2014): pp. 72–74.

Birdsall, Judd, "Sue Breeze on British Foreign Policy and Religion," *The Review of Faith and International Affairs* 12, no. 3, (2014): pp. 37–41.

Ferrara, Pasquale, "Reporting on religious freedom: the 'governmental' approach and the issue of legitimacy," in Pasquale Annicchino (ed.), *Protecting and Promoting Freedom of Religion or Belief in Foreign Policy. Which One?*, (EUI: San Domenico di Fiesole, 2013): pp. 59–65.

Foreign and Commonwealth Office, *Freedom of Religion or Belief. How the FCO Can Help Promote Respect for this Human Right*, 20/10/2016, available at: https://www.gov.uk/government/publications/freedom-of-religion-or-belief-how-the-fco-can-help-promote-respect-for-this-human-right.

Haynes, Jeffrey, *Faith-based Organisations and the United Nations*, ReligioWest working paper, RSCAS 2013/70, 2013.

Ministry of Foreign Affairs, "Roma: anche in Italia un osservatorio sulla libertà religiosa," 22/6/2012, available at: www.esteri.it/mae/it/sala_stampa/archivionotizie/approfondimenti/2012/06/20120622_roma.html

Ministry of Foreign Affairs, "Attacchi e violenze contro i cristiani-Terzi all'UE, applicare piano libertà religiosa," 27/11/2011, available at: www.esteri.it/mae/it/sala_stampa/archivionotizie/approfondimenti/2011/12/20111227_terziue.html

Terzi di Sant'Agata Giulio, *Intervento al Meeting Rimini 2012, Politica Internationale e Libertà Religiosa*, 24/8/2012, available at: www.meetingrimini.org/default.asp?id=673&item=5513.

Terzi di Sant'Agata Giulio, "Una forte azione politica e diplomatica a tutela della libertà religiosa," *L'Osservatore Romano*, 19/6/2012.

Thames, Knox, "Forging a Trans-Atlantic Partnership on Religious Freedom," The Review of Faith and International Affairs 12, no. 3, 2014, pp. 1–8.

Warsi, Sayeeda, "Le minacce alla libertà religiosa. Una crisi divenuta globale," *L'Osservatore Romano*, 11/1/2014.

Part III

Religious freedom as a foreign policy instrument

Problems and perspectives

7 A return to the collective aspect of religious freedom? Different religious perspectives on the construction of law

1. "Defamation of religions" at the United Nations

A few case studies can help us understand the difficulties that the United States (and European) model of protection and promotion of religious freedom encounter at the international level. This is the case with the conflict at the United Nations over resolutions on "defamation of religion,"[1] proposed and supported for many years by the Organization of the Islamic Conference, and also indicated, for example, as a case of particular importance by the 2014 report of the U.S. Commission on International Religious Freedom.[2] This issue is part of a difficult debate over the compatibility of the international conception of human rights with Islamic law,[3] as well as the positions of Muslim countries in the

[1] See Jeroen Temperman, "Religion and Free Speech at the United Nations: On the Crossroads of Politics, Secular and Religious Lobbies, and Judicial Expertise," *Quaderni di Diritto e Politica Ecclesiastica* 1, (2014): pp. 179–190. According to Temperman this issue is of fundamental importance in order to properly understand the wider context and debates on the international protection of religious freedom: "Going down the road of combating defamation of religion would be tantamount of destroying the core right of freedom of expression, but also the right to freedom of religion." *Ibid.*, p. 180. For a general introduction to the topic see Silvia Angeletti, "La diffamazione delle religioni nella protezione internazionale dei diritti umani," in David Brunelli (ed.), *Diritto penale e libertà religiosa* (Torino: Giappichelli, 2010), pp.149–195.

[2] US Commission on International Religious Freedom, *Annual Report 2014*, pp. 22–23 in which the role that the Commission has had at the United Nations is highlighted. According to Haynes this case shows the importance of this issues for states that adopt particularly discriminatory measures against religious minorities: "If intorduced, the laws, critics contended, were likely to be used unjustifiably to imprison those expressing anti-government opinions in Muslim countries, including journalists, students and other peaceful political dissidents. In addition, critics noted that the resolution championed by governments of countries with existing blasphemy laws, including: Iran, Pakistan and Egypt, might use the measure further to target already vulnerable religious minorities, including: Pakistan's Ahmadi Muslims, Bahai's in Iran and Christian Copts in Egypt." See Jeffrey Haynes, *Faith-based Organisations at the United Nations*, pp. 21–22.

[3] As Heiner Bielefeldt has underlined one has to take into account that within the Muslim world there are different conceptions and approaches to the issue of human rights: "[…] there is not *one* binding Islamic position but rather *a great variety* of 'Muslim voices' offering different views about whether and how the idea of human rights and Islamic normative requirement fit together." See Heiner Bielefeldt, "Muslim Voices in the Human Rights Debate," *Fides et Libertas* (2013): p. 31. Bielefeldt also recalls the abstention of Saudi Arabia in 1948 on article 18 of the Universal Declaration of Human Rights: "Saudi Arabia's abstension reflects the reluctance of a conservative Islamic government to endorse the emancipatory concept of human rights, a concept that is perceived to be alien and detrimental to the Islamic tradition." *Ibid.*, p. 44. For a general analysis see also Daniel Philpott, "Religious Freedom in Islam: A Global Landscape," *Journal of Law, Religion and State*, 2, (2013): pp. 3–21.

international arena in general.[4] These problems have already been pointed out, for example by Claudia Bianca Ceffa, who demonstrates that, despite the approval of the Arab Charter of Human Rights:

> [...] the Muslim countries are unable to overcome all the doctrines affirmed by classic Islamic jurisprudence (*fiqh*), which conceive the subjective law of the human being as community law and wholly divine, for which man cannot position himself as founder.[5]

As we will see, this position clearly had an immediate impact on the conception of and limits on the right of religious freedom as well.[6]

Every year, starting in 1999, the Organization of the Islamic Conference[7] has sponsored the adoption of certain resolutions on "defamation of religion,"[8] in which they express concern for the "growing phenomenon of intolerance and religious extremism and the intensification of a defamation campaign against religion and Islam in particular, of which the media provides a stereotypical and negative image."[9] As Silvia Angeletti points out, in many countries that are members of the Organization of the Islamic Conference, there are currently laws in effect that prohibit the criticism of religion[10] (in fact, they often only prohibit criticism of Islam). Starting in 1999, the Commission on Human Rights and subsequently the

4 This situation has become more difficult after the Arab Spring. See Andrea Locatelli and Vittorio E. Parsi (eds.), *L'onda lunga delle Primavere arabe*, (Milano: Vita e Pensiero, 2013) and also Michela Mercuri and Stefano M. Torelli (eds.), *La primavera araba* (Milano: Vita e Pensiero, 2012).

5 See. Claudia B. Ceffa, "La libertà religiosa nell'Islam: la Carta araba dei diritti dell'uomo," *Diritto e Religioni* 6, no. 11, (2011): p. 204.

6 Of particular importance could be for instance the absence of an explicit reference to the right to freely convert to another religion.

7 For an analysis of the role of this organization in the context of the approval of the resolutions on blasphemy, see Blandine Chelini-Pont, "La mobilisation de l'Organisation de la Conférence Islamique mondiale contre la diffamation de l'Islam (1999–2009) et ses consequences en France," *Annuaire Droit et Religions*, 4, (2009–2010): pp. 525–552 and also Blandine Chelini-Pont, "International Tug of War over the Defamation of Religion (1999–2009)," *Conscience and Liberty*, (2010): pp. 75–101.

8 See United Nations-Human Rights Commission, Resolution 1999/82, U.N. Doc. E/CN.4/1999/167, 30/4/1999; Resolution 2000/84, 26/4/2000, U.N. Doc. E/CN.4/2000/167; Resolution 2001/4, U.N. Doc. E/CN.4/2001/167, 18/4/2001; Resolution 2002/9, U.N. Doc. E/CN.4/2002/200, 15/4/2002; Resolution 2003/4, U.N. Doc. E/CN.4/2003/135, 14/4/2003; Resolution 2004/6, U.N. Doc. E/CN.4/2004/127, 13/4/2004; Resolution 2005/3, U.N. Doc. E/CN.4/2005/135, 12/4/2005 and also United Nations-Human Rights Council, Resolution 4/9, U.N. Doc. A/HRC/4/123, 30/3/2007; Resolution 7/19, U.N. Doc. A/HRC/7/78, 27/3/2008; Resolution 10/22, A/64/53, 26/3/2009; Resolution 13/16, U.N. Doc. A/HRC/RES/13/16, 25/3/2010; United Nations-General Assembly, Resolution 60/150, U.N. Doc. A/RES/60/150, 16/12/2005; Resolution 61/164, U.N. Doc. A/RES/61/164, 19/12/2006; Resolution 62/154, U.N. Doc. A/RES/62/154, 18/12/2007; Resolution 63/171, U.N. Doc. A/RES/63/171, 18/12/2008; Resolution 64/156, U.N. Doc. A/RES/64/156, 18/12/2009.

9 Silvia Angeletti, "Libertà d'espressione e libertà religiosa nei documenti delle Nazioni Unite: il concetto di diffamazione delle religioni è superato?", *Revista General de Derecho Canonico y Derecho Eclesiastico del Estado*, 26, (2011): p. 6.

10 As Silvia Angeletti argues: "For instance, the Algerian Penal Code prohibits insults against Islam or the Prophet Muhammad (art. 144 bis 2) [...] In Malaysia blasphemy and religious insults are prohibited in both the state-level Shari'a statutes and in federal law [...] Blasphemy laws can be found in the Pakistan Penal Code. They address a number of offences, including defiling a place of worship, defiling or damaging the Quran, insulting the Prophet Muhammand and apostasy," see Silvia Angeletti, "Defamations of Religion in UN Documents: Context and Trends," *Annuaire Droit et Religions*, 6, (2013): pp. 634–635.

United Nations Human Rights Council therefore adopted a series of resolutions, which were then confirmed by the vote of the General Assembly, expressing deep regret for the episodes of intolerance against the faithful of certain religions, and the negative (critical) stereotyping of certain religions, especially in the media. A characteristic element of these resolutions is the request for protection, not for the religious freedom of individuals or collectives of the faithful, but for abstract religious ideas, to immunize them from any critical discourse. The need for such protection is justified based on the contributions of these religions to modern civilization and the spread of values. The campaign for resolutions on "defamation of religions"[11] is central to the political and academic debate on the notion of the right of religious freedom in the international context. In this case, as Jeffrey Haynes has said: "Although it is not always considered to be very successful due to lack of coordination, the OIC has been attempting to institutionalise and represent Islam at the global level and is a major interlocutor with the European Union."[12] Legally, it seems all too easy to see how such resolutions clearly conflict with international instruments to protect human rights, in that it appears technically impossible to protect a mere abstract idea. Numerous objections have been raised against these proposals by non-governmental organizations and bodies representing numerous Christian denominations. If, on the one hand, these resolutions allow the construction of a legal screen defending Islam in Islamic majority countries, on the other hand, as we have seen, they can – precisely for this reason – be used as instruments of retaliation against the many communities which are almost always found to be minority denominations.

It should be pointed out, however, that some non-Muslim proponents have favorably welcomed the proposal of the Organization of the Islamic Conference. In October 2010, Cardinal Peter Turkson, then President of the Pontifical Council for Justice and Peace, attempt to advance the proposal for a new general resolution on religious freedom,[13] with the objective of addressing the content of resolutions on "defamation of religion," including them in a broader proposal of a resolution on religious freedom to "include Christianity, Christianophobia toward the religion and communities of believers in the Islamic world."[14]

11 See for an introduction Brett Scharffs, "International Law and the Defamation of Religion Conundrum," *The Review of Faith and International Affairs* 11, no. 1, (2013): pp. 66–75.

12 See Jeffrey Haynes, *Religious Transnational Actors and Soft Power* (Ashgate: Farnham, 2012), p. 55. In precedence Haynes has also underlined how it can be difficult for an organization such as the Organisation of the Islamic Conference to represent a unified position given the differences among the Member States: "In some respects, the, the OIC is very much like the UN: aspiration toward cooperation and achievement of collective goals are undermined by individual national interests concerns of leading countries. On the other hand, however, the OIC's shared religious and cultural focus has enabled it to carve out for itself a major role in international relations as a facilitator of mediation between conflicting Muslims groups, as in Somalia in the mid-2000s." *Ibid.*, p. 55.

13 Radio Vaticana, "Intervento del Cardinale Peter Kodwo Appiah Turkson, Presidente del Pontificio Consiglio della Giustizia e della Pace," 15/10/2010, available at: http://it.radiovaticana.va/articolo.asp?c=430815.

14 *Ibid.* Pope Francis, after the tragic events of January 7, 2015 when two terrorists killed some journalists of the French weekly *Charlie Hebdo* (accused of having been blasphemous) has said: "It is true that one should not react with violence, but if doctor Gasbarri (the organizer of papal trips that follows him) which is a friend, says something against my mother he deserves a punch! This is normal! One should not provoke. One should not insult the faith of the others. One should not make fun of religion." It is obvious that the Pope did not want to justify what happened in Paris, but it is interesting to notice that he wanted to signal that there should be a limit to the freedom of expression which should not be used to denigrate the faith of the others. See Luigi Accattoli, "L'invito di Papa Francesco a non deridere la fede degli altri," *Corriere della Sera*, 16/1/2015.

The acceptance of this proposal would have had counterproductive effects that are not in line with the national standards of protection of the right of religious freedom. As recalled by the United Nations Special Rapporteur for religious freedom, on the principles of the *Rabat Plan of Action*[15]:

> At the national level, blasphemy laws are counter-productive, since they may result in de facto censure of all inter-religious or belief and intra-religious or belief dialogue, debate and criticism, most of which could be constructive, healthy and needed. In addition, many blasphemy laws afford different levels of protection to different religions and have often proved to be applied in a discriminatory manner.[16]

The debates instigated by the presentation of resolutions to the United Nations have also been useful to support the formation of a European position on the subject, which from the beginning has been very critical of the initiatives of the Organization of the Islamic Conference. Similarly, the U.S. Commission on International Religious Freedom has expressed repeated criticisms of the initiatives[17] of the Organization of the Islamic Conference,[18] acting as a spokesperson for a true political and media campaign to close the vote against the various resolutions.[19]

Coordination among the countries of the European Union and the United States, in which the U.S. Commission on International Religious Freedom has played a role, seems to have borne its fruits with the approval of the 2011 resolution entitled *Combating Intolerance, Negative Stereotyping, and Stigmatization of, and Discrimination, Incitement to Violence against Persons Based on Religion or Belief*,[20] which avoids referring to the notion

15 United Nations-High Commissioner for Human Rights, *Rabat Plan of Action on the Prohibition of Advocacy of National, Racial or Religious Hatred that Constitutes Incitement to Discrimination, Hostility and Violence. Conclusions and Recommendations Emanating from the Four Regional Expert Workshops Organized by the OHCHR in 2011, and Adopted by Experts in Rabat, Morocco on October 2012*, available at: http://ohchr.org/documents/issues/opinion/seminarrabat/rabat_draft_outcome.pdf.

16 United Nations- General Assembly, *Report of the Special Rapporteur on Freedom of Religion or Belief*, 26/12/2013, A/HRC/25/58, par. 59.

17 See US Commission on International Religious Freedom, *The Dangerous Idea of Protecting Religions from "Defamation." A Threat to Universal Human Rights Standards*, Autumn 2010, available at: https://www.uscirf.gov/sites/default/files/resources/uscirf%20policy%20focus%20defamation%202010%20update.pdf and also the hearing of Leonard Leo, then Chair of the Commission before the Tom Lantos Human Rights Commission on 21/10/2009, available at: http://www.uscirf.gov/advising-government/congressional-testimony/testimony-uscirf-chair-leonard-leo-the-tom-lantos-huma-0. See also Robert George, "As UN Meets Apply Pressure against Blasphemy Law," *Christian Science Monitor*, 20/9/2013.

18 Already in 2009 the Council of the European Union had criticized the resolution highlighting how: "International human rights law protects individuals and groups of individuals and reiterate that 'defamation of religion' is not a human rights concept." See Council of the European Union, *Conclusions on Freedom of Religion or Belief*, 16/11/2009, doc. 15510/09.

19 According to the 2014 report of the Commission: "The State Department made defeating the defamation of religions resolutions a priority in its multilateral engagement: USCIRF and NGOs bolstered these efforts by highlighting the dangers of the resolutions through public advocacy campaigns and private meetings; and members of Congress did the same by writing UN delegations and heads of state urging them to vote against the resolutions." US Commission on International Religious Freedom, *Annual Report 2014*, pp. 22–23.

20 See United Nations-General Assembly, Resolution 66/167, U.N. Doc. A/RES/66/167, 19/12/2011; Resolution 67/168, U.N. Doc. A/RES/67/178, 20/12/2012.

of "defamation of religion"[21] in the text. However, the initiative of the Organization of the Islamic Conference is representative of the growing difficulties occurring on the international level in the attempt to pursue a unitary and shared notion of religious freedom. These difficulties, as we shall see, are not attributable to the activism of traditionally Muslim countries alone, but also to traditionally Christian countries.

2. The clash of traditional values vs. religious freedom: The role of the Orthodox Russian Church

In recent years the Russian Orthodox Church has emerged as a major protagonist in conflicts over the definition of the right of religious freedom at the international level. Its significance in this context can be seen in the various initiatives within international organizations, and in conflicts that have often set the Russian Federation (and the Russian Orthodox Church itself) against the United States and the countries of the European Union.

After the end of the communist regime, the Russian Orthodox Church attempted to reclaim a central role in the society and politics of the new state. The reconfiguration of the relationship between church and state occurred both through legislative changes in the context of the Russian constitutional framework and due to the restored central role of the Russian Orthodox Church in international relations.[22]

Some documents approved by the Russian Orthodox Church show that there has been a systematic theoretical development that, over the years, has led the Church and its positions to reclaim a role of greater relevance in Russian society. For example, The *Basis of the Social Concept of The Russian Orthodox Church*, approved by the Council of Bishops in August 2000, affirms the need for the renewed centrality of the Orthodox Church in Russian society and criticizes the language used by constitutional texts expressly recognizing the right to freedom of conscience:

> The appearance of the principle of freedom of conscience is a testimonial that, in the contemporary world, "public" religion becomes the "private" religion of the individual. In itself, this process attests to the disintegration of the system of spiritual values and the disappearance of the aspiration to salvation in most people who affirm the principle of freedom of conscience. If initially the state arose as sort of a tool of ratification of divine law in society, freedom of conscience transforms it definitively into an exclusively earthly institution, which has no religious obligations of any kind.[23]

21 According to Jeroen Temperman the issue needs still time to be fully overcome: "Although the content of the revamped Resolutions seemingly accords better with Western legal doctrine there remains a real sense of anxiety that these political resolutions will serve as justifications for national practices that unduly stifle speech critical of majority religions. The revamped consensus Resolution certainly does not take a strong stance against the countless suffocating blasphemy laws and policies that stifle all unpopular speech about religion." See Jeroen Temperman, "Religion and Free Speech at the United Nations: On the Crossroads of Politics, Secular and Religious Lobbies and Juridical Expertise," p. 180.

22 See Kristina Stoeckl, "The Human Rights Debate in the External Relations of the Russian Orthodox Church," *Religion, State and Society* 40, 2, (2012): pp. 212–232.

23 *Fondamenti della concezione sociale della Chiesa Ortodossa Russa*, 6, chapter III, quoted in Giovanni Codevilla, *Chiesa e Impero in Russia* (Milano: Jaca Book, 2011): p. 585.

Strong criticisms have been made against the proselytism of religious minorities, perceived as a true assault against the local Church. These positions of the Orthodox Church had a real influence on the application of the regulations of the Russian Federation governing the treatment of religious groups. It is no coincidence that the European Court of Human Rights has repeatedly declared Russia to be in violation of the Convention for its treatment of certain minority religions.[24] Essentially, despite the formal constitutional guarantees offered to minority religious groups, the material constitution indicates a regime that in reality is averse to religious freedom, where there is a "supremacy of one religion that leads to tolerance toward other churches and denominations and the intolerance of others."[25] Politically, according to Giovanni Codevilla, the Russian Orthodox Church has put itself into a position of apparent supremacy, even over the state:

> Today the Orthodox Church, despite the destruction suffered under Bolshevism, appears to possess internal strength and credibility greater than that of the state, especially with regard to popular legitimacy, and is therefore capable of dictating its own conditions for the support it grants to political power.[26]

Clearly it must be admitted that the state also has an influence on the Church and its instrumentalization. For example, Alicja Curanović identifies in the relationship between temporal power and spiritual power a clear pre-eminence of the latter, indicating that often "traditional religions" are called upon to support the political decisions of the government and support them in their pastoral action.[27] With the fall of the Communist regime, the Russian Orthodox Church therefore seems to have found a new vitality. For the purposes of our analysis, it seems relevant to examine how the conception of human rights and the right of religious freedom developed by the Russian Orthodox Church has influenced and is influencing the development of international norms, also taking into account the renewed conflicts in which the Russian Federation is the protagonist.

The Basis of the Social Concept of The Russian Orthodox Church already contains a significant reference to the conception of human rights that proceeds from recognition of the concept of *dignitas humana* "rooted in the biblical affirmation of man as *imago Dei*, from which follows that the exercise of rights cannot be separated from moral law and the aim of the good of the person and of society."[28] It is explicit, as we have previously seen, in its condemnation of the principle of freedom of conscience, perceived as a true attack on the public role of religion. It also asks for formal recognition of the primacy of the Russian

24 See, among the others, the following decisions of the European Court of Human Rights: *Krupro and others v. Russia* (26587/07), 26/6/2014 and *Church of Scientology of St. Petersburg and others v. Russia* (47191/06), 27/10/2014.

25 Giovanni Codevilla, *Chiesa e Impero in Russia*, p. 602.

26 *Ibid.*, p. 604.

27 As Alicja Curanović underlines: "'Traditional religions' are expected to legitimate the Kremlin's actions whether it concerns the policy in Chechnya, Putin's third presidential term or Russia's cordial relations with Iran. If the Kremlin loses its confidence in a religious organisation's dedication, it can abruptly reduce benefits." See Alicja Curanović, *The Religious Diplomacy of the Russian Federation*, IFRI, Rusiia/NIS Center, Report, n. 12, June 2012, p. 8, available at: www.ifri.org/?page=contribution-detail&id=7198.

28 Giovanni Codevilla, "Ortodossia e linguaggio sui diritti umani in Russia. Nuovo legame tra religione e politica," *Stato, Chiese e Pluralismo confessionale*, (February 2009): p. 3.

Orthodox Church over other religious denominations[29] and stresses the centrality of the Church in the construction of national identity.[30]

Critical and fearful of an excessively liberal development in the interpretation and application of human rights, it appears that the Russian Orthodox Church fundamentally aspires to be a state religion, or at least a "soft state religion," where only a few minimal rights are guaranteed to religious minorities, and the majority Church is placed in a position of pre-eminence.[31] This theoretical and political paradigm has profound implications for the conceptualization of human rights by the Russian Orthodox Church, which subsequently has repercussions on state policy, both domestic and international. Giovanni Codevilla, who has built a detailed argument based on theories of human rights by the Russian Orthodox Church, refers to the *Declaration of Human Rights and Dignity* approved on April 10, 2001 by the World Russian People's Council, which explicitly establishes the subordination of human rights to religious values:

> There are values that are placed above human rights. These are values such as faith, morality, relics or shrines (*svjatyni*), and the Fatherland (*Otečestvo*). When these values and the realization of human rights come into conflict, society, state, and law must harmoniously reconcile. Situations cannot be allowed where the realization of human rights tramples on faith and moral tradition, offends religious or national sentiments, venerated relics or shrines, or threatens the existence of the Fatherland (*Otečestvo*). We see that there is a danger of "invention" of "rights" that legalize behavior condemned by traditional morals and all historical religions.[32]

This approach, particularly with regard to freedom of conscience, was then confirmed in the conciliatory document *The Russian Orthodox Church's Basic Teaching on Human Dignity, Freedom and Rights*, drafted under Patriarch Cyril I and approved on June 26, 2008.[33]

29 At point 4 of chapter III it is underlined that: "[...] the Russian Orthodox Church, being part of the only universal Church of Christ, shall have a public legal status superior to the one of the other religions of the Russian state. This status it is due to the Church as it is the 'sacre supreme reality' for the major part of the Russian population and a significative historical force in the creation of the Russian state." Quoted in Giovanni Codevilla, *ibid.*, p. 3.

30 Also on this point it is possible to find explicit references: "The patriotism of the Christian orthodox must be efficient. It is based on the defence of the homeland from the enemy, in the work for the good of the nation, in making any effort in the organization of the life of the people also through the participation to the running of the State. The Christian is called to protect and promote national culture and the self-conscience of the people. The Nation, civil or ethnic, when is totally or in major part an orthodox mono-confessional community can be considered as a single community of faith: an orthodox nation." Quoted in Giovanni Codevilla, *ibid.*, pp. 4–5.

31 On this point see also Alicja Curanović, "Relations between the Orthodox Church and Islam in the Russian Federation," *Journal of Church and State* 52, no. 3, (2010): pp. 503–539.

32 Quoted in Giovanni Codevilla, *Ortodossia e linguaggio sui diritti umani in Russia. Nuovo legame tra religione e politica*, p. 8.

33 In the 2008 document there is a specific reference to the issue of freedom of conscience: "Sometimes freedom of conscience is understood as indifference of the State and society or as a request of religious neutrality. Certain ideological interpretations of the right to religious freedom insist on the necessity to recognise that all the religions are 'equally true.' This is not acceptable for the Church which, while respecting the freedom of choice, is called to witness the truth of which it is a custodian and to underline the errors." Quoted in Giovanni Codevilla, *ibid.* p. 11.

Contrary to the content of the constitutional text of the Russian Federation,[34] the picture that emerges from the documents on human rights produced by the Russian Orthodox Church show the desire to create a close connection between church and state, where the protection of human rights is subordinated to religious values, as interpreted by the hierarchy of religious power. In this sense, there appears to be increasing evidence of a newly-regained vigor in the idea of a historical salvational mission, entrusted to Russia in the name of all the Slavic people, of a true

> [...] plan-Slavic messianism which aspires, as it once did, to carry the Orthodox cross of salvation to all Slavs in the territories of the former Soviet empire, to those scattered throughout the world, as well as other peoples inclined to accept it.[35]

It is clear that in the face of this theoretical construction of human rights, and of relations between the state and religious groups, the pluralistic principle that is one of the cardinal principles of international instruments (above all in the jurisprudence of the European Court of Human Rights) with regard to the subject of religious freedom[36] is destined to come into profound conflict with the legal system of the Russian Federation, and more generally with the theoretical scaffolding upon which the system is based.

Another interesting aspect for the purposes of our analysis is to see how this limiting and limited construction of the right of religious freedom (and of conscience) is used by the Russian Orthodox Church not only to influence legislative (and jurisprudential) developments within the system of the Russian Federation, but how it is now positioned as the central theoretical paradigm in order to exercise an influence on the construction of the right of religious freedom within multilateral organisms and international law. This strategy obviously also represents the other side of the coin of a renewed activism of the Russian Federation on the international policy scene.[37]

The activities of the Russian Orthodox Church on the international scene can be traced particularly to the action of the Church Department for External Affairs, whose influence has grown considerably under the guidance of Cyril I,[38] and the coordination of the Foreign

34 According to article 14 of the Constitution of the Russian Federation: "1. The Russian Federation is a secular state. No religion may be established as a state or obligatory one. 2. Religious associations shall be separated from the State and shall be equal before the law."

35 Giovanni Codevilla, "Ortodossia e linguaggio sui diritti umani in Russia. Nuovo legame tra religione e politica," p. 12.

36 On this issue see Aernout Nieuwenhuis, *The Concept of Pluralism in the Case Law of the European Court of Human Rights*, European Constitutional Law Review, 3, 2007, pp. 367–384 and also Zachary Calo, "Pluralism, Secularism and the European Court of Human Rights," *Journal of Law and Religion*, 26, (2010–2011): pp. 261–280. The conflict between the Russian legal order and the principle of pluralism is underlined also by Giovanni Codevilla: "From the exclusive link between the Church and the Nation and between Orthodoxy and patriotism follows that pluralism is considered as a crumbling element of society." Giovanni Codevilla, *ibid.*, p. 13.

37 See Alicja Curanović, *The Religious Factor in Russia's Foreign Policy* (New York-London: Routledge, 2012).

38 As Kristina Stoeckl notices under the guidance of Cyril I the activities of the Department have increased: "[...] in 2011, the Representation of the Russian Orthodox Church to the European Institutions was founded, followed in 2004 by a Permanent Mission to the Council of Europe in Strasbourg. Kirill and his collaborators in the Department for External Relations kept the human rights question on the agenda of the Russian Orthodox Church and under Kirill's leadership the Department became the centre for the Russian Orthodox human rights debate, coordinating and collecting both the internal and the

Minister of the Russian Federation, who often acts as spokesperson for proposals that are the result of the work of the bodies of the Russian Orthodox Church.

The start of cooperation in this area can be traced to the creation of a working group initiated by Patriarch Alexy II in 2003.[39] Among the results of the working group, which helped to develop a strategy to strengthen the contribution of religion in the international context, was the official proposal to create a special consultative forum, to include global religious leaders.[40] This initiative was then presented to the United Nations, with the cooperation of the countries of the Organization of the Islamic Conference, with the aim of ensuring a greater role for religion in international relations. In this case as well, as Robert Blitt says, the Russian choice was to privilege traditional religions, excluding all minority religions.[41] The documents and the approach of the Russian Orthodox Church with regard to the protection of human rights, and specifically the right of religious freedom, demonstrate a deliberate attempt to denounce an international system perceived as culturally hegemonized by the discourse on rights in a Western context and which deliberately excludes "traditional values."

At least two examples of this approach can be mentioned. The first is the Russian position regarding resolutions on "defamation of religions," repeatedly approved at the United Nations, which have always seen the Russian Federation aligned with the positions of the Organization of the Islamic Conference.[42] The second is the attempt to obtain UN approval of the resolution entitled *Promoting Human Rights and Fundamental Freedoms Through a Better Understanding of Traditional Values of Humankind*, which was immediately criticized and rejected by some countries such as Norway and France.[43] Despite the criticisms

external communication on this topic." See Kristina Stoeckl, "The Human Rights Debate in the External Relations of the Russian Orthodox Church," p. 214.

39 See Robert C. Blitt, "Russia's 'Orthodox' Foreign Policy: The Growing Influence of the Russian Orthodox Church in Shaping Russia's Policies Abroad," *University of Pennsylvania Journal of International Law*, 33, no. 2, 2011, pp. 363–460. As Blitt highlights, the cooperation between religious and civil powers is fostered also through the creation of a network of NGOs, such as the *Russkiy Mir Foundation*, with a specific goal: "Orthodoxy shall be promoted not only under the banner of an ostensibly more inclusive notion of spirituality or culture, but also as part of the government's broader effort to safeguard the Russian language. Taking a deeper look at Russkiy Mir's most recent interactions with the Russian Orthodox Church, it becomes obvious that the relationship is intensifying as the foundation drifts away from its core mission of promoting the Russian language and wanders into the realm of endorsing an exclusively Orthodox version of spirituality and Russia abroad." *Ibid.*, p. 387.

40 This proposal has been explicitly made by the Russian Minister for Foreign Affairs Sergej Lavrov in 2007: "Spiritual values of all world religions make it imperative to achieve inter-civilizational accord and fight manifestations of xenophobia and racism [...] We propose [...] establishing under the United Nations auspices, a special forum – a kind of consultative Council of Religions – for the exchanges of views among representatives of major confessions." Intervention at the 11th meeting of the plenary session of the General Assembly quoted in Robert C. Blitt, *ibid.*, p. 397.

41 According to the Russian paradigm only the Russian Orthodox Church can deliver the spiritual capital necessary to the presence of the State in the international arena: "Even within the ostensibly open-ended context of an interreligious dialogue, 'nontraditional' religions are a priori excluded, and other so-called non-Orthodox 'traditional' faiths must channel their views through the filter of the Moscow Patriarchate," Robert C. Blitt, *ibid.*, p. 399.

42 This common position on the resolutions is highlighted by Robert Blitt: "Russia's U.N. mission consistently has voted in favor of defamation resolutions in the U.N. General Assembly and Human Rights Council, even going so far to endorse new restrictions on the right to freedom of expression, despite such limitis being unrecognized by the International Covenant on Civil and Political Rights." *Ibid.*, p. 441.

43 The activism of the Russian Orthodox Church has increased especially after 2008 often in coordination with other initiatives of the Russian Federation. As Kristina Stoeckl points out: "[...] the Human Rights Doctrine is the product of a tradition of Church diplomacy that goes back to Soviet times and that is

and distancing of some states, the Russian Federation succeeded in organizing a seminar in Geneva, during which some ideas at the foundation of the draft resolution were discussed, and the resolution was then subsequently approved without the vote of the Western countries.[44] The explicitly-declared Russian objective is to break the Western "ideological monopoly" on the theory and application of human rights, perceived as overly individualistic, and strengthening a more communitarian conception which is strongly influenced by the contribution of religious denominations – the Russian Orthodox Church above all.[45] This last conception, as evidenced by Cyril I, has immediate concrete effects, that is, the rejection of any discussion on abortion, homosexuality, euthanasia, and other third-generation rights considered to be in deep conflict with religious teachings.[46] A situation is then created where a state that declares itself to be secular ends up promoting a kind of religious sectarianism in the realm of its foreign policy.[47] It therefore appears to overturn the traditional paradigm, wherein the right of religious freedom is a useful instrument for minorities to protect themselves from potentially oppressive majorities.[48] In this scenario, religious

characterized by close coordination between the Church and the state, an overlapping of interests, and strategic alliances-building with likeminded religious and secular actors in the West." See Kristina Stoeckl, *The Russian Orthodox Church and Human Rights*, p. 106. On the resolutions approved at the United Nations see also Christopher McCrudden, *Human Rights, Southern Voices and "Traditional Values" at the United Nations*, University of Michigan Public Law Research Paper No. 149, May 2014, available at: http://papers.ssrn.com/sol3/papers.cfm?abstract_id=2474241.

44 On March 24, 2011 the Human Rights Council of the U.N. approved a resolution (16/3) through which it asked to the Advisory Committee to draft a report. This study was coordinated by prof. Vladimir Kartashkin and made public on December 12, 2011. A following resolution (21/3) was approved on September 27, 2012 by the Human Rights Council.

45 All the different steps that led to the approval of the resolution have been detailed by Kristina Stoeckl. According to her the debate on "traditional values" is the attempt to drastically think again the very same meaning and notion of human rights: "The example of the traditional values debate in the United Nations Human Rights Council clearly shows that the Russian government and the Moscow Patriarchate coordinated their efforts in pushing through an anti-liberal human rights agenda. Both actors emphasized repeatedly that human rights should not be 'monopolized' by a Western liberal and secular interpretation [...] The Russian government wants a multipolar international system without the constraints of a supranational legal order based on human rights, and it does not want international interference in its domestic politics. The Patriarchate, on the other hand, wants to prevent the extension of human rights into areas of family and private law, and it wants to seal off Russian society from 'harmful' liberalization and pluralization." See Kristina Stoeckl, *The Russian Orthodox Church and Human Rights*, p. 113.

46 According to Patriarch Cyril I: "The (Orthodox) religious tradition [...] contains a criterion for discerning good from evil. From the perspective of this tradition, the following cannot be accepted as normative: mockery of sacred things (i.e. blasphemy), abortion, homosexuality, euthanasia and other actions that are actively advocated today by the concept of human rights." See Interfax, "Metropolitan Kirill of Smolensk and Kaliningrad: Human Rights and Moral Responsibility," 4/4/2006, available at: www.interfax-religion.com/?act=document&div=62.

47 This attempt is highlighted by Robert Blitt, especially in the context of the relationships of the Russian Orthodox Church with other religious groups: "The consequences of this partnership have serious implications at the international level, manifested in efforts to supplant universal human rights norms and legitimate the rationale that certain select 'traditional' or 'major' religion merit greater influence in the formulation of international rules than others." See Robert C. Blitt, "Russia's 'Orthodox' Foreign Policy: The Growing Influence of the Russian Orthodox Church in Shaping Russia's Policies Abroad," p. 459.

48 See Alexander Agadjanian, "Liberal Individual and Christian Culture: Russian Orthodox Teaching on Human Rights in Social Theory Perspective," *Religion, State & Society* 38, no. 2, (2010): pp. 97–113. This position has been for instance advocated by the representative of the Russian Orthodox Church at the Council of Europe: "It is also unjust when International religious freedom advocacy refers to religious

freedom becomes above all a tool in the hands of the majority religion to protect the privileged position granted to it by the legal system.

With this approach in mind, is not surprising to note how many times the reports of the U.S. Commission on International Religious Freedom and the Department of State were criticized by members of the Russian Federation or the Russian Orthodox Church, which considered them partial and largely drafted in the sole interest of US foreign policy.[49] Similarly, one cannot marvel at the inclusion of Russia among the countries being monitored and for which 2014 report of the U.S. Commission on International Religious Freedom noted severe violations. The report, in addition to noting the favorable treatment of the Russian Orthodox Church, lists numerous violations of the fundamental rights of Jehovah's Witnesses and Muslims.[50]

The positions of the US government, and the bodies entrusted to promote religious freedom based on the International Religious Freedom Act, are often antithetical to those of the Russian Federation and the Russian Orthodox Church. Thus their agreement on intent and positions with regard to the situation of Christian minorities in the Middle East can hardly be surprising. As we have seen, this topic has been the center of attention of both the United States and the European Union. The Russian Federation played a central role in opposing a military operation in Syria against the government of Bashar al-Assad, who was accused of persecuting political minorities. One of the arguments used to oppose this intervention was related to the possible consequences on Christian minorities deemed better protected in the context of a political regime hegemonized by the Alawites of President Assad.[51] The crisis of the Iraqi political regime and the rise of the forces of the "Islamic State" have led the foreign relations departments of the Moscow Church to approve a document entitled *Mass Terror Against the Christians of Iraq*, which condemns the persecutions of Christian minorities.[52]

freedom only in the sense of the protection of religious minorities. Religious freedom does not exist in the abstract and pure form. It is always embodied in a particular individual way." See Hegumen Philip Ryabyk, "New Challenges to Religious Freedom in Europe," in Pasquale Annicchino (ed.), *Freedom of Religion or Belief in Foreign Policy. Which One?*, p. 21.

49 See Interfax, "Moscow Patriarchate Expects Future Reports of the USA Department of State Will Be More Objective," 25/11/2010, available at: www.interfax-religion.com/?act=news&div=7955. The article quotes Philip Ryabyk, according to which: "I'd like to wish that in the future the report will have truly equal, friendly attitude to various religious organizations and will avoid selectiveness so that religious situation is reflected more fully."

50 The report lists many of these violations: "New 2012 laws and 2014 amendments to the anti-extremism law were used against religious individuals and groups particularly Jehovah's Witnesses and Muslim readers of Turkish theologian Sais Nursi." See US Commission on International Religious Freedom, *Annual Report 2014*, p. 141. On the situation in Russia it is also worth pointing at the report written by the Commission after a visit to the country in 2013. See US Commission on International Religious Freedom, *Unruly State of Law. Findings from a Visit of the U.S. Commission on International Religious Freedom*, January 2013. The introduction to the report summarizes well the findings of the Commission: "Overall, religious freedom conditions in Russia continue to deteriorate. Chronic serious problems highlighted in previous USCIRF report remains, including the application of the religion law and the use of the anti-extremism law against peaceful religious groups and individuals." *Ibid.*, p. 1.

51 See Ellen Barry, "Russian Church is a Strong Voice Opposing Intervention in Syria," *The New York Times*, 31/5/2012.

52 Department of External Relations of the Russian Orthodox Church, "Mass Terror Against the Christians of Iraq," 14/8/2014, available at: https://mospat.ru/it/2014/08/14/news106827.

Thus, while on many topics of the international agenda we see a conflict between a certain interpretation of religious freedom and other fundamental rights (such as the rights of lesbian, gay, bisexual, transgender, and intersexual minorities), on the topic of persecutions against Christians, we see a growing closeness between certain Western positions and those of the Russian Orthodox Church.[53] As we have seen, the Russian Orthodox Church positions itself as a major actor in the context of international disputes over religious freedom. This prominence is even greater considering the position of the Russian Federation, which perceives the promotion of religious freedom by the United States (and the European Union) as a true act of imperialism.

3. US Catholic Constitutionalism and the defense of "*Libertas Ecclesiae*"

Although it is possible to trace a "hegemony of religious freedom"[54] in US public discourse, at the same time we must also point out, for the purposes of this work, how strongly developments and reflections regarding policy on religious freedom, particularly in the context of US Catholicism,[55] has influenced the creation of new multilateral and national institutions whose primary activity is to protect this right. For example, the influence of conceptions of religious freedom developed in the United States appear evident when we analyze the path that led to the approval of the Universal Declarations of Human Rights, or the Declaration on Religious Freedom, *Dignitatis Humanae*, approved during the Second Vatican Council.[56]

[53] This has been confirmed also by Metropolitan Hilarion in 2012 in a lecture given at Villanova University in the United States. It is worth pointing at the passaged of the lecture referring to the resolutions adopted by the European Union: "In Iraq only a tenth of a million-and-a-half Christian population that lived there ten years ago has survived. In Egypt we are witness to a mass exodus of Christians. There are practically no Christians left in Lybia. Ninety five percent of Christians have abandoned Homs is Syria. We, Orthodox and Catholics, must raise our voices jointly in defense of Christians subjected to persecution and repression in the aforementioned countries, as well as in Afghanistan, Pakistan, India, Indonesia, the Philippines, Nigeria and in a number of other countries [...] The countries of Europe have traditionally defended the interests of Christians, for example, in the Middle East or in Far Eastern Asia. In the present circumstances we hope that the resolution adopted by the European Parliament on 20 January 2011 on the position of Christians in the context of religious freedom, as well as the declaration of the Committee of Foreign Ministers of the European Union on 22 February, will have practical consequences. They were a result of active participation of the Christian Churches in this direction. We hope that the USA will join us in the defense of Christians." See Department of External Relations of the Russian Orthodox Church, "Metropolitan Hilarion Lectures at Villanova University in the USA," 1/11/2012, available at: https://mospat.ru/en/2012/11/01/news74213. See also European Centre for Law and Justice, *The Persecution of Oriental Christians, What Answers from Europe?*, January 2011, available at: https://eclj.org/pdf/ECLJ_ReportantiChristianpersecution20110120.pdf.

[54] Elizabeth Shakman Hurd, "The Hegemony of Religious Freedom," *The Globe and Mail*, 17/10/2012.

[55] Allen D. Hertzke, "Roman Catholicism and the Faith-Based Movement for Global Human Rights," *The Review of Faith and International Affairs*, 3, no. 3, 2009, pp. 19–24.

[56] In particular on Vatican II, see Thomas F. Farr, "Religious Realism in Foreign Policy: Lessons from Vatican II," *The Review of Faith and International Affairs* 3, no. 3, (2005): pp. 25–34. For Thomas Farr: "Filtered through the work of Jesuit theologian John Courtney Murray, the American understanding of religious freedom and its place in the nation's democratic experiment helped to inform the Council Fathers in developing the Church's doctrine of human freedom in civil society, and its view of proper role of government in addressing the religious dimension of individual and social life." *Ibid.*, p. 25. On the genesis and drafting of the declaration see also Silvia Scatena, *La fatica della libertà. L'elaborazione della Dichiarazione "Dignitatis Humanae" sulla libertà religiosa del Concilio Vaticano II* (Bologna: Il Mulino, 2004).

The fundamental criterion that has guided the contribution of US Catholicism has often been an inclusive and plural approach to the notion of religious freedom, with the aim of supporting religious voices in public debate and individual faith choices with respect to social environments considered hostile. The developments in the Islamic world and with the Russian Orthodox Church, analyzed above, attest to how, on the international level, one of the principal elements of pressure for a reworking of religious freedom to give greater emphasis to the collective and institutional dimensions comes from some of the major religious traditions. Although the criticism of a conception of human rights deemed overly individualistic and Western is clear in the case of Islam and the Russian Orthodox Church, it is also important to address some positions of US Catholic scholars, who bear witness to a lively and present tension within that country, which is perhaps more representative of the Western world and which, as we have seen, has protected and promoted religious freedom as one of the pillars of its foreign policy. This development is not only the result of decisions regarding US foreign policy, but is also influenced by the development of the jurisprudence of the US Supreme Court on the subject of religious freedom.

One of the most important developments in US Catholicism can be seen in the events taking place in the heart of so-called "Catholic constitutionalism,"[57] a term by which Susanna Mancini refers to the scholars and authors involved in the "Catholic conservative" movement. One who certainly bears mentioning is Robert George, formerly a Commissioner on the U.S. Commission on International Religious Freedom, and formerly Chairman.[58] In his writings, Robert George has often emphasized that the right of religious liberty should be conceived not solely in the acceptance of the right to worship, but should be understood as a right with an explicit public dimension, connected not so much the notion of individual autonomy as to that of conscience, understood as the capacity of individual to take on and fulfill moral obligations.[59] Notable as well are the positions of John Finnis, who, in criticizing the approach of Christopher Eisgruber and Lawrence Sager, who expressed approval of the Supreme Court ruling in the *Smith* case, has pointed out that the right of religious freedom merits a specific protection that differentiates it

57 See Susanna Mancini, *Un affare di donne. L'aborto tra libertà eguale e controllo sociale* (Padova: CEDAM, 2013), p. 141.

58 According to Susanna Mancini, Robert George is one of the intellectual leaders of this movement as: "[...] it is widely known Robert P. George, Princeton professor, defined by the New York Times as 'the most important conservative intellectual of the country' exercises a growing influence on Conservative thinking. This influence is connected to the rediscovery of Catholic natural law as a foundational premise for constitutional law." *Ibid.* p. 142. To this extent the influence of George's thinking goes beyond Catholicism to affect also other religious groups: "George's 'Catholic constitutionalism' has been well received also by other christian and non-christian religious groups as one can see from the text of the 'Manhattan Declaration' of 2009, promoted by different Christian leaders and drafted by George. The Declaration focuses on three moral fundamental issues, not taking into account any particular religious belonging: human dignity, connected to protection of life since conception, marriage between people of different sexes as a natural institution and the defense and protection of religious freedom." *Ibid.*, p. 143.

59 As Robert George writes: "The right to follow one's conscience, and the obligation to respect conscience, especially in matters of faith, where the right of conscience takes the form of religious liberty of individual and communities of faith obtain not because people as autonomous agents should be able to do as they please; they obtain, and are stringent and sometimes overriding, because people have duties and the obligation to fulfill them." See Robert George, "What is Religious Freedom?", *Catholic Exchange*, 7/8/2013, available at: http://catholicexchange.com/ehat-is-religious-freedom. See also Robert George, *Conscience and its enemies: Confronting the dogmas of liberal secularism* (Wilmington: Intercollegiate Studies Institute, 2013).

from other human rights.[60] Paolo Carozza, often close to the positions of the Magisterium on the topic of religious freedom, has pointed out the danger of a unidirectional interpretation of human rights, overly influenced by a purely individualistic dimensional aspect, particularly in the international sphere.[61] In his interpretation, the centrality of a reconstruction of religious freedom is fundamental, taking into consideration the moral and ontological bases that are part of the essentially religious nature of the human experience.[62]

Many of these positions can be traced to the influence of the teachings of Benedict XVI, who often made explicit reference to the same arguments maintained by these authors, and at the beginning of *Libertas Ecclesiae*, stressed the necessity of an understanding of the right of religious freedom which includes a collective institutional dimension as well. Within this paradigm, religious freedom must necessarily include the "possibility for the church to be itself, to live and express in full autonomy and without impediment its cultural and ethical originality, freely exercising its spiritual mission among humanity."[63] It was precisely during the pontificate of Benedict XVI that there was a recovery of the principle of *Libertas Ecclesiae* and its renewed centrality. As Fabio Franceschi points out:

> [...] with the commitment of the Pope, who was prolific in fighting the increasingly widespread idea widespread – which will always continue to spread – of modernity as emancipation from religion in contemporary society, which is the case in Western countries where the secularization and laicization process of institutions is more advanced.[64]

Therefore, it is upon the religious freedom of the Church that all other fundamental freedoms may be constructed:

> [...] the safeguarding of *libertas ecclesiae* is, then, perceived as the indispensable condition for defending and promoting the freedom of the human person and of peoples, as

60 See John Finnis, *Why Religious Liberty is a Special, Important and Limited Right*, Notre Dame Law School Legal Studies Research Paper No. 09–11, October 2008. Available at: http://goo.gl/sCj6WL. For a general understanding of Eisgruber's and Sager's position see Christopher L. Eisgruber and Lawrence G. Sager, *Religious Freedom and the Constitution* (Cambridge: Harvard University Press, 2010).

61 Paolo Carozza offers an interpretation very critical of the practices at the international level speaking of "oligarchies" that support particular conceptions of human rights: "The world of human rights thus sometimes resembles a tightly drawn oligarchy, in which dissent and difference are strictly limited. And like in many other oligarchic systems, a well-financed effort to advance a particular right or rights can be quite effective because there is a relatively narrow elite that needs to be influenced." See Paolo Carozza, "The Right and the Good and the Place of Freedom of Religion in Human Rights," *Communio: International Catholic Review*, 40, (2013): p. 8.

62 For Paolo Carozza the right to religious freedom is to be recognized as fundamental and basic also for other human rights: "Without an understanding of human rights that places the religious sense of man (as individual and in community) at the center, the other freedoms do not make sense and are destined ultimately to be subordinated to some imposition of power or another (...) In particular, human rights risk becoming the tools of a totalizing control rather than the expression of the human heart's structural longing for freedom." Ibid., p. 15. For an analysis focused on Catholicism see Paolo Carozza and Daniel Philpott, "The Catholic Church, Human Rights and Democracy: Convergence and Conflict with the Modern State," *Logos* 15, no. 1, (2012): pp. 15–43. Other interesting arguments are made by Mary Ann Glendon, former US Ambassador to the Holy See and former member of the US Commission on International Religious Freedom. See Mary A. Glendon, "Religious Freedom: A Second Class Right?"

63 Fabio Franceschi, "Libertà della Chiesa e laicità dello Stato nell'insegnamento di Benedetto XVI," *Diritto e Religioni* 6, no. 12, (2011): p. 138.

64 *Ibid.*, p. 139

> well as to indicate the direction of formulation, theoretical and practical, of an authentic social democracy. By defending its own freedom, the Church defends the human person, their dignity and their fundamental rights.[65]

The reconstruction of a religious freedom not understood merely as the right to individual freedom, but as a broader right which includes a collective institutional dimension, can also be seen in the pronouncements of the United States Conference of Catholic Bishops. In this regard, we can refer to the document *Our First, Most Cherished Liberty: A Statement on Religious Freedom*.[66] This document lists the phenomena perceived by the United States Conference of Catholic Bishops as violations of religious freedom. One of the major items on this list is the healthcare reform promoted by President Obama, which obligates religious institutions to provide drugs considered to be in conflict with Church teachings.[67] The document strives to point out the close connection between protection of religious freedom in the United States and the ability to protect and promote this right in other parts of the world:

> If religious liberty is eroded here at home, American defense of religious liberty abroad is less credible. And one common threat, spanning both the international and domestic arenas, is the tendency to reduce the freedom of religion to the mere freedom of worship. Therefore, it is our task to strengthen religious liberty at home, in this and other respects, so that we might defend it more vigorously abroad.[68]

According to this interpretation, only a notion of religious freedom strongly anchored in its collective and institutional aspects, not just the individual, is capable of ensuring the success of the US initiative to promote religious freedom. Thomas Farr, who more than any other author has closely followed the developments in the actual application of the International Religious Freedom Act, has often pointed out the significance of the public dimension of religion and its possible effects in the context of US foreign policy. In his view, only if we are ready to recognize this public dimension of the religious factor, without relegating it to the merely private sphere, will it be possible to understand the true possible scope of the policies for promotion of religious freedom which the United States has decided to undertake through the approval of the International Religious Freedom Act, and ensure that their full potential is expressed. According to Thomas Farr, US policies have been ineffective precisely because, over the years, officials called upon to apply the US regulation have denied the public role of religion. A promotion of religious freedom that conceives this right only in its private individual dimension and not in its collective and institutional dimension would therefore be unable to ensure an effective and robust protection of the right of religious freedom:

> It is thus sadly ironic that the American Founders' understanding of religious freedom which influenced Father Murray's work, and through him *Dignitatis Humanae*, has largely been abandoned by the American political class. What now pervades

65 *Ibid.*, p. 141.

66 U.S. Catholic Bishop's Conference, *Our First, Most Cherished Liberty. A Statement on Religious Freedom*, 2012, available at: http://goo.gl/CpAJyE.

67 From this point of view the *Hobby Lobby* decision is of fundamental importance.

68 US Catholic Bishop's Conference, *Our First, Most Cherished Liberty. A Statement on Religious Freedom*, p. 9.

> U.S. academic, judicial, and policy discourse is a thin and fragile view of religion as mere personal preference, and religious freedom as a privatized right with little legitimate connection to democratic public policy.[69]

The effort of the authors, who can be included in the notion of "Catholic constitutionalism" coined by Susanna Mancini, consists in the desire to emphasize the necessary relational[70] and institutional[71] dimensions of the concept of religious freedom. Substantially, on the one hand they criticize secularization and the increasingly marginal role of religion in Western society, and on the other they point out how this phenomenon has influenced the theorization of the right of religious freedom, and in the emphasis of the individual dimension above all, to the detriment of the collective and institutional dimensions. According to Thomas Farr, this paradigm must be fully re-thought, because it has influenced everybody who has been tasked with creating policies to promote the right of religious freedom and apply the norms of the International Religious Freedom. As Thomas Farr writes:

> The "privatization" assumption has been absorbed like mother's milk by almost the entire range of those groups composing the foreign policy establishment. That spectrum includes the realists, the liberal internationalists, and, perhaps to a lesser degree, even the neoconservatives.[72]

The assumption of the privatization of the religious phenomenon and the related criticism from authors such as Thomas Farr, and in general from authors who are part of "Catholic constitutionalism," demonstrate how the definition of a legal notion of religious freedom is now influenced by developments from religious groups that highlight the need for greater consideration for the institutional and collective dimension of this right. The position of these authors, who are largely American, is particularly significant from the perspective of our work, as it demonstrates how criticisms of Western policies of promotion of religious freedom, perceived as too favorable to an overly individualistic notion, come not only from religious traditions such as Islam or the Russian Orthodox Church, but are also present in the United States.

69 Thomas F. Farr, "Religious Realism in Foreign Policy: Lessons from Vatican II," p. 25.

70 This is for instance the position advocated by Allen Hertzke: "[…] religion is relational, and true freedom of faith must protect the right of people to gather in communities of belief for mutual expression and succor. Indeed, religious communities are historically and ontologically 'prior' to the modern state and their autonomy deserves protection from overreaching political authorities." Allen D. Hertzke, "Religious Freedom in the World Today: Paradox and Promise," in Mary A. Glendon, Hans F. Zacher, (ed.), *Universal Rights in a World of Diversity. The Case of Religious Freedom*, p. 112.

71 See in this case the position of David Novak in David Novak, *In Defense of Religious Liberty* (Wilmington: ISI Books, 2009).

72 Thomas F. Farr, *Religious Realism in Foreign Policy: Lessons from Vatican II*, p. 29. In concluding his analysis Farr advocates a major role and a better comprehension of the religious factor: "An increasing role for religious freedom and religious communities in the U.S. foreign engagement will of course be fraught with challenges and pitfall. But it would be the height of irresponsibility to continue America's current privatization driven inertia on matters of religion and foreign policy." *Ibid.*, p. 33.

References

Accattoli, Luigi, "L'invito di Papa Francesco a non deridere la fede degli altri," *Corriere della Sera*, 16/1/2015.

Agadjanian, Alexander, "Liberal Individual and Christian Culture: Russian Orthodox Teaching on Human Rights in Social Theory Perspective," *Religion, State & Society* 38, no. 2, (2010): pp. 97–113.

Angeletti, Silvia, "Defamations of Religion in UN Documents: Context and Trends," *Annuaire Droit et Religions*, 6, (2013): pp. 634–635.

Angeletti, Silvia, "Libertà d'espressione e libertà religiosa nei documenti delle Nazioni Unite: il concetto di diffamazione delle religioni è superato?," *Revista General de Derecho Canonico y Derecho Eclesiastico del Estado*, 26, (2011): pp. 1–16.

Angeletti, Silvia, "La diffamazione delle religioni nella protezione internazionale dei diritti umani," in David Brunelli (ed.), *Diritto penale e libertà religiosa* (Torino: Giappichelli, 2010), pp.149–195.

Barry, Ellen, "Russian Church is a Strong Voice Opposing Intervention in Syria," *The New York Times*, 31/5/2012.

Bielefeldt, Heiner, "Muslim Voices in the Human Rights Debate," *Fides et Libertas*, (2013): pp. 31–57.

Blitt, Robert C., "Russia's 'Orthodox' Foreign Policy: The Growing Influence of the Russian Orthodox Church in Shaping Russia's Policies Abroad," *University of Pennsylvania Journal of International Law*, 33, no. 2, 2011, pp. 363–460.

Calo, Zachary, "Pluralism, Secularism and the European Court of Human Rights," *Journal of Law and Religion*, 26, (2010–2011): pp. 261–280.

Carozza, Paolo, "The Right and the Good and the Place of Freedom of Religion in Human Rights," *Communio: International Catholic Review*, 40, (2013): pp. 1–17.

Carozza, Paolo, and Philpott, Daniel, "The Catholic Church, Human Rights and Democracy: Convergence and Conflict with the Modern State," *Logos* 15, no. 1, (2012): pp. 15–43.

Ceffa, Claudia B., "La libertà religiosa nell'Islam: la Carta araba dei diritti dell'uomo," *Diritto e Religioni* 6, no. 11, (2011): pp. 202–221.

Chelini-Pont, Blandine, "International Tug of War over the Defamation of Religion (1999–2009)," *Conscience and Liberty* (2010): pp. 75–101.

Chelini-Pont, Blandine, "La mobilisation de l'Organisation de la Conférence Islamique mondiale contre la diffamation de l'Islam (1999–2009) et ses consequences en France," *Annuaire Droit et Religions*, 4, (2009–2010): pp. 525–552.

Codevilla, Giovanni, *Chiesa e Impero in Russia* (Milano: Jaca Book, 2011).

Codevilla, Giovanni, "Ortodossia e linguaggio sui diritti umani in Russia. Nuovo legame tra religione e politica," *Stato, Chiese e Pluralismo confessionale*, (February 2009): pp. 1–23.

Curanović, Alicja, *The Religious Factor in Russia's Foreign Policy* (New York-London: Routledge, 2012).

Curanović, Alicja, *The Religious Diplomacy of the Russian Federation*, IFRI, Russia/NIS Center, Report, n. 12, June 2012, available at: www.ifri.org/?page=contribution-detail&id=7198.

Curanović, Alicja, "Relations between the Orthodox Church and Islam in the Russian Federation," *Journal of Church and State* 52, no. 3, (2010): pp. 503–539.

Department of External Relations of the Russian Orthodox Church, "Mass Terror Against the Christians of Iraq," 14/8/2014, available at: https://mospat.ru/it/2014/08/14/news106827.

Department of External Relations of the Russian Orthodox Church, "Metropolitan Hilarion Lectures at Villanova University in the USA," 1/11/2012, available at: https://mospat.ru/en/2012/11/01/news74213.

Eisgruber, Christopher L., and Sager, Lawrence G., *Religious Freedom and the Constitution* (Cambridge: Harvard University Press, 2010).

European Centre for Law and Justice, *The Persecution of Oriental Christians, What Answers from Europe?*, January 2011, available at: https://eclj.org/pdf/ECLJ_ReportantiChristianpersecution20110120.pdf.

Farr, Thomas F., "Religious Realism in Foreign Policy: Lessons from Vatican II," *The Review of Faith and International Affairs* 3, no. 3, (2005): pp. 25–34.

Finnis, John, *Why Religious Liberty is a Special, Important and Limited Right*, Notre Dame Law School Legal Studies Research Paper No. 09–11, October 2008. Available at: http://goo.gl/sCj6WL.

Franceschi, Fabio, "Libertà della Chiesa e laicità dello Stato nell'insegnamento di Benedetto XVI," *Diritto e Religioni* 6, no. 12, (2011): pp. 136–167.

George, Robert, "As UN Meets Apply Pressure against Blasphemy Law," *Christian Science Monitor*, 20/9/2013.

George, Robert, "What is Religious Freedom?," *Catholic Exchange*, 7/8/2013, available at: http://catholicexchange.com/ehat-is-religious-freedom.

George, Robert, *Conscience and its enemies: Confronting the dogmas of liberal secularism* (Wilmington: Intercollegiate Studies Institute, 2013).

Glendon, Mary A., "Religious Freedom: A Second Class Right?," *Emory International Law Review* 61, (2012): pp. 971–990.

Haynes, Jeffrey, *Faith-based Organisations and the United Nations*, ReligioWest working paper, RSCAS 2013/70, 2013.

Haynes, Jeffrey, *Religious Transnational Actors and Soft Power* (Ashgate: Farnham, 2012).

Hearing of Leonard Leo, Chair of the Commission before the Tom Lantos Human Rights Commission on 21/10/2009 available at: www.uscirf.gov/advising-government/congressional-testimony/testimony-uscirf-chair-leonard-leo-the-tom-lantos-huma-0.

Hegumen Philip, Ryabyk, "New Challenges to Religious Freedom in Europe," in Pasquale Annicchino (eds.), *Freedom of Religion or Belief in Foreign Policy. Which One?* (EUI Press: San Domenico di Fiesole, 2013): pp. 21–25.

Hertzke, Allen D., "Roman Catholicism and the Faith-Based Movement for Global Human Rights," *The Review of Faith and International Affairs*, 3, no. 3, 2009, pp. 19–24.

Hertzke, Allen D., "Religious Freedom in the World Today: Paradox and Promise," in Mary A. Glendon, and Hans F. Zacher, (ed.), *Universal Rights in a World of Diversity. The Case of Religious Freedom.*

Interfax, "Moscow Patriarchate Expects Future Reports of the USA Department of State Will Be More Objective," 25/11/2010, available at: www.interfax-religion.com/?act=news&div=7955.

Interfax, "Metropolitan Kirill of Smolensk and Kaliningrad: Human Rights and Moral Responsibility," 4/4/2006, available at: www.interfax-religion.com/?act=document&div=62.

Locatelli, Andrea, and Parsi Vittorio E (eds.), *L'onda lunga delle Primavere arabe* (Milano: Vita e Pensiero, 2013).

Mancini, Susanna, *Un affare di donne. L'aborto tra libertà eguale e controllo sociale*, (Padova: CEDAM, 2013).

McCrudden, Christopher, *Human Rights, Southern Voices and "Traditional Values" at the United Nations*, University of Michigan Public Law Research Paper No. 149, May 2014, available at: http://papers.ssrn.com/sol3/papers.cfm?abstract_id=2474241.

Mercuri, Michela, and Torelli, Stefano M. (eds.), *La primavera araba* (Milano: Vita e Pensiero, 2012).

Nieuwenhuis, Aernout, *The Concept of Pluralism in the Case Law of the European Court of Human Rights*, European Constitutional Law Review, 3, 2007, pp. 367–384.

Novak, David, *In Defense of Religious Liberty* (Wilmington: ISI Books, 2009).

Philpott, Daniel, "Religious Freedom in Islam: A Global Landscape," *Journal of Law, Religion and State*, 2, (2013): pp. 3–21.

Radio, Vaticana, "Intervento del Cardinale Peter Kodwo Appiah Turkson, Presidente del Pontificio Consiglio della Giustizia e della Pace," 15/10/2010, available at: http://it.radiovaticana.va/articolo.asp?c=430815.

Scatena, Silvia, *La fatica della libertà. L'elaborazione della Dichiarazione "Dignitatis Humanae" sulla libertà religiosa del Concilio Vaticano II* (Bologna: Il Mulino, 2004).

Scharffs, Brett, "International Law and the Defamation of Religion Conundrum," *The Review of Faith and International Affairs* 11, no. 1, (2013): pp. 66–75.

Shakman Hurd, Elizabeth, "The Hegemony of Religious Freedom," *The Globe and Mail*, 17/10/2012.

Stoeckl, Kristina, "The Human Rights Debate in the External Relations of the Russian Orthodox Church," *Religion, State and Society* 40, 2, (2012): pp. 212–232.

Stoeckl, Kristina, *The Russian Orthodox Church and Human Rights* (London-New York: Routledge, 2014).

Temperman, Jeroen, "Religion and Free Speech at the United Nations: On the Crossroads of Politics, Secular and Religious Lobbies, and Judicial Expertise," *Quaderni di Diritto e Politica Ecclesiastica* 1, (2014): pp. 179–190.

United Nations – General Assembly, *Report of the Special Rapporteur on Freedom of Religion or Belief*, 26/12/2013, A/HRC/25/58.

United Nations – High Commissioner for Human Rights, *Rabat Plan of Action on the Prohibition of Advocacy of National, Racial or Religious Hatred that Constitutes Incitement to Discrimination, Hostility and Violence. Conclusions and Recommendations Emanating from the Four Regional Expert Workshops Organized by the OHCHR in 2011, and Adopted by Experts in Rabat, Morocco on October 2012*, available at: http://ohchr.org/documents/issues/opinion/seminarrabat/rabat_draft_outcome.pdf.

U.S. Catholic Bishop's Conference, *Our First, Most Cherished Liberty. A Statement on Religious Freedom*, 2012, available at: http://goo.gl/CpAJyE.

U.S. Commission on International Religious Freedom, *Annual Report 2014*.

U.S. Commission on International Religious Freedom, *Unruly State of Law. Findings from a Visit of the U.S. Commission on International Religious Freedom*, January 2013.

U.S. Commission on International Religious Freedom, *The Dangerous Idea of Protecting Religions from "Defamation." A Threat to Universal Human Rights Standards*, Autumn 2010, available at: https://www.uscirf.gov/sites/default/files/resources/uscirf%20policy%20focus%20defamation%202010%20update.pdf

8 The impossibility of religious freedom?

1. The impact of the International Religious Freedom Act

As we have seen, some years after its approval in 1998, the International Religious Freedom Act has been an example of legislation that has inspired many Western countries to make the protection and promotion of the right of religious freedom an objective of their foreign policy. It remains to be seen, however, what the actual impact of this instrument has been. It is certainly appropriate to point out that the International Religious Freedom Act has inspired new academic reflections by legal and political scholars, who have investigated the new projection of the right of religious freedom into the international context. Although some have emphasized the inherent danger of unilateral action in defense of a specific right, others have emphasized the parallel inefficacy of these same international and multilateral institutions.

The evidence needed to verify the impact of the International Religious Freedom act can be derived from the June 2013 hearing held at the U.S. House of Representatives.[1] Thomas Farr, who has followed the developments of US policy from the start, both as an academic and, for a time, as director of the Office of International Religious Freedom at the Department of State, offered a rather negative assessment of the US experience over these seventeen years:

> Notwithstanding the hard, creative work of the State Department's Office of International Religious Freedom, it would be difficult to name a single country in the world over the past fifteen years where American religious freedom policy has helped to reduce religious persecution or to increase religious freedom in any substantial or sustained way.[2]

To substantiate his interpretation of the US experience, Thomas Farr cites the continually growing data on religious persecutions and restrictions of the exercise of religious freedom

[1] This aspect is highlighted by Thomas Farr in his intervention before the House of Representatives: "The policy mandated by the 1998 International Religious Freedom Act (IRFA) has now been in operation for fifteen years. This is the first and only Congressional oversight hearing in those fifteen years concerning the operation of IRFA." See Thomas F. Farr, *Testimony before the House Committee on Oversight and Government Reform-Subcommittee on National Security* within the context of the hearing *Examining the Government's Record on Implementing the International Religious Freedom Act*, 13/6/2013.

[2] *Ibid.*

in the world. He points to cases of non-application of the norms and penalties set out by the International Religious Freedom Act:

> Some of these countries have been on the IRFA-mandated list of particularly severe violators, the so-called "countries of particular concern." IRFA requires that this list be issued annually but the Obama administration has not done so since 2011. Congress, it seems, takes little notice of this [...] IRFA permits economic sanctions against the nations on this list, but in fifteen years only one country has ever been sanctioned.[3]

The responsibility for the meager results obtained by the application of a regulation considered lacking and lax could be attributed to the lack of attention paid to the topic by the major government organs and agencies.[4] Thomas Farr, though pointing out some positive initiatives, criticizes the absence of a true strategy to promote religious freedom, especially with regard to the Muslim world. This approach, in his interpretation, is the child of the traditional skepticism that has been demonstrated over the years by many parties with regard to the significance of the religious factor in US foreign policy[5]: "It seems to me that a significant proportion of our foreign policy officials no longer believe that religious freedom is the 'first freedom' – of American history, of the US constitution, and of all people everywhere. "[6]

Thomas Farr therefore takes the position of US "Catholic constitutionalism," traditionally also held by other religious movements that oppose the advancement of secularization in Western society and the interpretation of religion as a merely private matter.[7] The promotion of the right of religious freedom has therefore become, in his interpretation, one of the many US policies for the promotion of human rights that is often balanced with other rights often considered to be in conflict with it, as is the case with the rights of the lesbian, gay, bisexual, transgender, and intersexual communities.[8] Similarly, Thomas Farr views the terminology used by the European institutions (freedom of religion or belief) as a relativization of the right of religious freedom, since the term "belief" is too vague and weakens the

3 *Ibid.*

4 According to Thomas Farr: "None of the three administrations responsible for IRFA have adapted a robust view of the law and policy it mandates. Each has assumed a narrow, highly rhetorical approach – characterized by reports, lists of severe persecutors that have little effect, and a State Department activity known as "rising the issue" with governments (an activity which should not be confused with "solving the problem"), *ibid.*, p. 4.

5 Thomas Farr lists a series of possible causes for the failure of the implementation of the International Religious Freedom Act: "For example, there is some evidence of a generalized sense among our diplomats that a vigorously pursued religious freedom policy would be unconstitutional. Some believe the policy imposed by Christians and is designed to clear the way for Christian missionaries. Some conservatives are hesitant to support religious freedom for Muslims around the world." *Ibid.*, p. 6.

6 *Ibid.*, p. 7.

7 The position is made clear by the same Thomas Farr during the hearing: "Many of our political and foreign policy leaders today, however, see religious freedom as a private matter, with few legitimate public purposes. For some, religious liberty is in no sense *necessary* to individuals and societies. Rather, it is merely one in an ever growing list of rights claims. In this case a claim of privilege by religious people. As such it warrants no special protection, but must be 'balanced' against all other claims." *Ibid.*, p. 7.

8 Thomas Farr has criticized many times the Obama administration for this reason. See Thomas F. Farr, "Obama Administration Sidelines Religious Freedom Policy" and George Weigel, "Why U.S. International Religious Freedom Policy Fails," *Catholic Exchange*, 6/8/2013.

effective protection and promotion of the right of religious freedom.[9] In fact, Farr himself criticizes the use of this terminology in some State Department documents.[10] Criticisms of Thomas Farr are not isolated, but represent a platform of arguments often shared by those who had greater expectations for the potential of the International Religious Freedom Act and the US action and protection of religious freedom. These positions are opposed by people such as Elizabeth Shakman Hurd, who maintain that the United States does, and has done, too much already and that its action, often unilateral, is nothing more than the result of an internal political agenda. This agenda is then translated into foreign policy actions that can often end up damaging religious minorities.

So while Thomas Farr believes that the United States has done too little in comparison with what was promised with the entry into force of the International Religious Freedom Act, Elizabeth Shakman Hurd believes that the idea of a special regulation to protect and promote the right of religious freedom is problematic in itself. Essentially, she argues, this regulation is being used solely to globally project the narrative of US exceptionalism:

> These U.S. efforts reflect and reproduce a long-standing American prophetic tradition in which, as Talal Asad argues, "democracy" and "human rights" are "integral to the universalizing moral project of America – the project of redeeming the world – and an important part of the way America sees itself." IRFA [International Religious Freedom Act – Ed.] is part of «America's narrative of redemption that is being applied globally.[11]

The promotion of this right, as Elizabeth Shakman Hurd points out, is not merely the result of political pressures from religious movements, but also of those arising from liberal individualism.[12] These policies are therefore substantiated in the exportation of a kind of nationalism based on the promotion of the religious freedom that forms the basis of US identity:

> IRFA is the latest expression of a long-standing American nationalist narrative in which a state-sponsored commitment to free and healthy religion is seen as benefitting not

9 The statement by Farr during the hearing on this point is telling: "One of the characteristics of the European privatization project, notes Oxford University Professor Roger Trigg, is its willful dilution of religious freedom to a right to 'freedom of religion or belief'. The problem is that 'belief' can mean virtually anything one feels strongly about, from environmentalism to the Manchester soccer club. Religion in Europe has long since lost any special status in law, society and politics, and is now routinely treated as merely one human preference among an infinite possible number of preferences." Thomas F. Farr, *Testimony before the House Committee on Oversight and Government Reform-Subcommittee on National Security* within the context of the hearing *Examining the Government's Record on Implementing the International Religious Freedom Act*, p. 8.

10 He does so by making reference to the 2012 report on international religious freedom: "It is therefore a cause of alarm to see the following sentence at the beginning of the 2012 State Department Annual Report, in a section describing why this right is important for the United States: "Freedom of religion and belief and the right to worship as one chooses fulfill a deep and abiding human need'," *ibid.*, p. 8.

11 Elizabeth Shakman Hurd, "Religious Freedom, American-style," pp. 236–237.

12 Elizabeth Shakman Hurd identifies different groups: "These includes liberal legal internationalists and human rights advocates who stand for individual rights and freedom of choice, advocacy groups for whom some form of Christianity serves as the foundation of human rights, democracy and freedom. American nationalists for whom the 'city on a hill' narrative presupposed by these projects resonates with long-standing ideals of American exceptionalism and the sacralization of the American national project, and missionaries for whom religious liberalization signals an openness to their missions that may have not existed, or was felt differently, in earlier times." *Ibid.*, p. 237.

only Americans but also the rest of the world, by saving them from religious and political tyranny.[13]

Elizabeth Shakman Hurd's criticism in other writings is quite crushing. Indeed, she describes initiatives for the protection and safeguarding of religious freedom in the international arena as actual "mind control" that has now become a "global enterprise."[14] Neither argument appears to fully describe what has occurred since 1998 with the approval of the International Religious Freedom Act. It is difficult to refuge Thomas Farr's view that the application of the 1998 regulation has been partial, or in some cases even absent. A good example of this is the case of Indian Prime Minister Narendra Modi, who in 2005 was denied an entry visa to the United States, where he was due to appear as a participant in an event organized by the Hindu community in New York.[15]

The US government justified its decision to sanction Narendra Modi based on the presumed role he played in the extremely serious conflicts in 2002, which set Hindus against Muslims in the Indian state of Gujarat. According to the State Department, Modi did not do everything in his power to prevent the massacre. As of today, according to the State Department, Narendra Modi is the only foreign political representative who has ever been denied entry to the United States based on the International Religious Freedom Act.[16] Beyond the peculiarity of the case, it is interesting to note how, according to some, the application of the sanction against Modi was actually based on a precise political decision of the State Department, aimed at having the US action be perceived as a protection of religious freedom not just for Christian communities, but all communities, and in this specific case, the Muslim community.[17] However, the 2014 election of Narendra Modi as Prime Minister of India revealed the limited nature of the actual applicability of such sanctions (in this case, through diplomatic immunity). Narendra Modi was then allowed to speak and hold political meetings in large US cities and to meet major US political representatives.[18]

Although Thomas Farr's argument reveals a node of critical importance with regard to the effectiveness of regulations, it must be noted that Farr himself seems to adhere to the premises of US exceptionalism, which too often has justified the failure of the United States to comply with the obligations of cooperation in multilateral institutions and the search for

13 *Ibid.*, p. 238.

14 See Elizabeth Shakman Hurd, "Believing in Religious Freedom," *The Immanent Frame*, 1/3/2012, available at: http://blogs.ssrc.org/tif/2012/03/01/believing-in-religious-freedom.

15 Narendra Modi, at that time *Chief Minister* of the State of Gujarat, started his political career in the conservative Hindu party Rashtriya Swayamsevak Sangh (RSS). He owes his political success to political campaigns focused on Hindu nationalism and Hindu traditional values often used against the Muslim minority of the country (13 percent of the total population).

16 This is the reconstruction of the facts offered by J. Mann, according to which: "The State Department invoked a little-known U.S. law passed in 1998 that makes foreign officials responsible for 'severe violations of religious freedom' ineligible for visas. Mr. Modi is the only person ever denied visa to the U.S. under this provision, U.S. officials confirm." James Mann, "Why Narendra Modi was Banned from the U.S.," *The Wall Street Journal*, 2/5/2014.

17 *Ibid.*

18 See Shreeya Sinha, "Indian Leader Narendra Modi, Once Unwelcomed in U.S., Get Rock Star Reception," *The New York Times*, 27/9/2014. As Ellen Barry writes: "As it became clear that Mr. Modi was likely to become prime minister, the United States has sought to set that history aside, build a relationship with him and use the change of governments to deepen both trade and defense cooperation with India." See Ellen Barry, "U.S. Court Issues Summons to Modi Lawsuit Over 2002 Riots," *The New York Times*, 26/9/2014.

instruments that could lead to the involvement of a greater number of countries in actions to protect the right of religious freedom. This position is problematic in an increasingly pluralistic world with a growing number of actors who put forth varying conceptions of the right of religious freedom.

The critical position of Elizabeth Shakman Hurd, on the other hand, does not properly take into account Thomas Farr's arguments on the relative effectiveness of the regulation and the sparse empirically verifiable results.[19] Elizabeth Shakman Hurd has, in fact, opposed international initiatives for the promotion and protection of religious freedom and the consequent development of specialized institutions, as they are influenced by a notion of religious freedom that claims to be universal, but instead reproduces those that are typically US-centric: "Religious freedom needs to be reimagined as a site of resistance against powerful authorities, rather than a form of discipline imposed by them, funneling people into predefined religious boxes and politicizing their differences."[20] Elizabeth Shakman Hurd's critical theory appears to be well-founded, but excessive compared to the actual impact of the International Religious Freedom Act. The 2014 report of the U.S. Commission on International Religious Freedom makes some important points that demonstrate an only partial application of the regulation.[21] As the Commission itself concludes:

> Because of the indefinite waivers for Saudi Arabia and Uzbekistan, the United States has not implemented a unique policy response tied to the CPC [Countries of Particular Concern – Ed.] designation for either country. The other actions expired on August 18, 2013, when two years elapsed without their renewal. As a result, there currently is not a single IRFA specific sanction in place for particularly severe violations of religious freedom.[22]

2. Circulation of the model

Despite problems with the effective application of the norms of the International Religious Freedom Act, and criticisms coming from within the United States from both academia and policymakers, in recent years an increasing number of states, and the European Union itself, have been inspired by the US legislation. In addition to the European examples we previously covered, we should certainly address the policies and institutions of the Canadian government. The Government of Canada actually decided to include the protection and

19 On this point it is worth pointing at what has been said by Katrina Lantos Sweet, former Chair of the US Commission on International Religious Freedom: "[...] the flexibility provided in IRFA has proven detrimental to the intent of the law. Generally, no new Presidential actions pursuant to Country of Particular Concern designations have been levied, with State Department instead relying on pre-existing sanctions." Katrina Lantos Sweet in her interventions also mentions many other factors that contributed to the lack of the full implementation of the IRFA provisions. See Katrina Lantos Sweet, *Testimony Before the National Security Subcommittee of the House Committee on Oversight and Government Reform* within the context of the hearing *Examining the Government's Record on Implementing the International Religious Freedom Act*, 13/6/2013. For a technical analysis see US Government Accountability Office, *Report to Congressional Committees-International Religious Freedom Act. State Department and Commission are Implementing Responsibilities but Need to Improve Interaction*, GAO-13-196, March 2013, pp. 1–66, available at: www.gao.gov/products/GAO-13-196.

20 Elizabeth Shakman Hurd, *The Hegemony of Religious Freedom*.

21 See US Commission on International Religious Freedom, *Annual Report 2014*, pp. 14–19.

22 *Ibid.*, p. 19.

promotion of religious freedom as one of the priorities of its foreign policy. On February 19, 2013, Prime Minister Stephen Harper announced the establishment of "Canada's Office of Religious Freedom," simultaneously appointing Andrew P. Bennett to be Ambassador for Religious Freedom. In this case as well, numerous observers have noted that in fact greater attention is paid to Christian communities, to the detriment of other religious minorities.[23] Others have noted that it is not the Canadian government's job to promote religious freedom beyond its own borders or to give special attention to this right alone, to the detriment of a global and all-inclusive approach to human rights.[24]

The idea of creating such an office did not originate with the government of Stephen Harper, but was already present in the 1998 program of Jean Chretien, precisely during the period when the United States approved the International Religious Freedom Act.[25] The events related to the situation in Pakistan had particular significance, since the assassination of the Minister for Religious Minorities, Shahbaz Bhatti, was an important influence on Stephen Harper's decision.[26] The office was established with an initial budget of five

23 For instance Arvind Sharma has defined the creation of the office as an act of "predatory Christian proselytization." See Arvind Sharma, "Religious Freedom, Compliments of the West," *The Mark News*, 6/12/2011. For a review of the different positions taken in this debate see Robert Joustra, "Three Rival Versions of Religious Freedom: What Canada's Office of Religious Freedom Can Teach Us About Principled Pluralism," *The Review of Faith and International Affairs* 12, no. 3 (2014): pp. 41–44. The Canadian Prime Minister, in order to reply to some of his critics, decided to symbolically present the initiative in a Jama'at of the Ahmadiyya Muslim Community in Toronto. As James Wallace and Richelle Weisman highlight: "The Ahmadiyya Muslim community has experienced significant persecution in some Muslim-majority countries, such as Pakistan, where it is viewed as a heretical Muslim sect. By having the public announcement at the Ahmadiyya mosque, Prime Minister Harper sought to confront one of the major criticism directed at the office even before it was formalized that the ORF would only address the persecution of Christians around the world and would ignore other faiths." James C. Wallace and Richelle Wiseman, "The Promise of Canada's Office of Religious Freedom," *The Review of Faith and International Affairs* 11, no. 3 (2013): p. 52.

24 Some of the critiques have been addressed by Stephen Harper immediately on the day of the launch of the initiative. According to him the original initiative was not launched to protect only Christian communities, but the goal was to promote and protect religious freedom for everybody. Ambassador Andrew Bennett resonated along the same lines: "This is not about a theological question – it's about a human issue, not a theological issue. So all religions, all people of faith and again those who choose not to have faith need to be protected. So it's promoting that mandate." *Ibid.*, p. 55. The Minister for Foreign Affairs John Baird underlined the same aspect in a speech at the United Nations in September 2011: "I am pleased to report that Canada will be creating an Office of Religious Freedom within our Government at the heart of my own department. The office will promote freedom of religion and freedom of conscience as key objectives of Canadian foreign policy. The long history of humanity has proven that religious freedom and democratic freedom are inseparable." See John Baird, "Address to the United Nations General Assembly," 26/9/2011, available at: www.international.gc.ca and also John Baird, "Address at Office of Religious Freedom Stakeholder Consultation," 3/10/2011, available at: www.international.gc.ca.

25 Lloyd Axworthy, former Minister for Foreign Affairs and International Trade, proposed the creation of the office that did not materialize. Then, in 2004, a parliamentary resolution was approved. The resolution asked the government: "[...] to make the protection and promotion of the right to freedom of religion and belief a central element of its efforts to defend human rights internationally." See James C. Wallace and Richelle Wiseman, "The Promise of Canada's Office of Religious Freedom," p. 53. This connection with parallel developments in the United States alarmed more secular Canadian politicians. As argued by Robert Joustra: "American connections to the Office of Religious Freedom buttress the concerns of laicists, who worry that American-style religious freedom is really a project of Judeo-Christian proselytization in disguise." See Robert Joustra, "Three Rival Versions of Religious Freedom: What Canada's Office of Religious Freedom Can Teach Us About Principled Pluralism," p. 46.

26 The correlation is well explained by James Wallace and Richelle Wisemann: "[...] on March 26, 2011, Canada's Governor General dissolved parliament and dropped the election writ, setting the stage for

million Canadian dollars and a five-person staff, including the Ambassador for Religious Freedom.[27] Despite further progress made in Parliament,[28] the initiative did not survive once the Stephen Harper government was dissolved.

One of the first initiatives undertaken by the Canadian office was the establishment of a Religious Freedom Fund, to finance specific projects aimed at promoting religious freedom. The first initiatives were carried out in Nigeria and some countries in Central Asia.[29] As in the case of the United States and other countries that have undertaken similar initiatives, it will be important to assess the level of consistency that will be maintained in reporting violations of religious freedom in countries that are important commercial partners of Canada, such as China.[30]

In the Canadian case as well, therefore, we see the influence of the US experience. But the countries that have been inspired to this model have not slavishly repurposed the regulatory and institutional structure of the International Religious Freedom Act. Some have attempted to differentiate their policies, aiming not at the promotion of religious freedom, but the need to have specific institutions dedicated to the weaving of political relations with religious leaders, who are perceived as increasingly significant actors. This is the case

Canada's 36 day federal election campaign. During the campaign, when Harper declared his intention to create the ORF at a Coptic Christian church, standing by his side was Peter Bhatti, the brother of Shahbaz Bhatti." See James C. Wallace and Richelle Wiseman, "The Promise of Canada's Office of Religious Freedom," p. 58. The killing of Shahbaz Bhatti has a significant impact on many countries. Also in the United States, Leonard Leo, then Chair of the US Commission on International Religious Freedom underlined the relevance of the event: "The assassination earlier this year in Pakistan of two high-ranking government officials for their opposition to blasphemy laws reminded us of how violent religious extremism and religious freedom violations are destabilizing a critical partner, creating a climate of impunity by fueling hatred and violence against both Muslims and non-Muslims in that country." Leonard Leo and Don Argue, "International Religious Freedom: Why It matters and How to Protect It," *International Affairs Review* 20, no. 1 (2011): p. 2.

27 Also in this case some commentators have underlined how the budget allocated to the office is far from sufficient for an enterprise on a global scale and seems to respond more to logics of political marketing: "The Harper Conservatives' latest brainchild, an ambassador for religious freedom, is supposed to criticize other countries' lack of protection for religious minorities. These critiques will have zero effect on the intended targets, but they will be wildly popular with domestic religious groups, who are the real political targets." Jeffrey Simpson, "The Office of Religious Freedom, More Conservative Slice and Dice," *The Globe and Mail*, 23/2/2013.

28 In April 2013 a parliamentary resolution was approved, with the endorsement of the five major parties, calling for international action for the promotion and protection of religious freedom. For James Wallace and Richelle Wiseman this was a further confirmation of the relevance of the topic for Canadian institutions: "This unanimous vote by the Canadian Parliament is a bold declaration to the International community that religious freedom is a priority for Canada foreign policy, in the present and for the future, no matter which party forms the government." James C. Wallace and Richelle Wiseman, "The Promise of Canada's Office of Religious Freedom," p. 59.

29 Laura Payton, "Canada Giving $ 1.2M for Religious Freedom in Nigeria, Central Asia," *CBS News*, 26/8/2013, available at: http://en.africatime.com/external?url=http://www.cbc.ca/news/politics/story/2013/08/26/pol-office-of-religious-freedom-projects.html.

30 Chinese diplomats have immediately criticized the initiative of the Canadian government: "Already, China, a key trading partner, has registered concern about the office. Mr. Bennett said he seeks a constructive dialogue with Beijing, but doesn't think Zhang Junsai, the Chinese ambassador to Canada, was pleased to learn he plans to meet with critics such as Tibetan Buddhist," Steven Chase, "New Religious-freedom Watchdog Faces Uphill Battle," *The Globe and Mail*, 7/6/2013. The relationship and dialogue with China on the topic of religious freedom has been of fundamental importance also for the United States, see Jason Kindopp, "Principled Engagement in China," *The Brandywine Review of Faith and International Affairs* 1, no. 1 (2003): pp. 21–30.

in France, for example. Others, such as Italy, despite the influence it had in the process that led to the approval of the European guidelines, created some institutions and proposed some policies which were not supported consistently, given the constant alternation of governments. The United Kingdom appears to be the European country that is most consistently creating positive institutional synergies between Parliament and the Foreign and Commonwealth Office to ensure the effective application of measures for the promotion of religious freedom.

Despite the US influence on European models, significant differences remain, including with regard to terminology. Thus, while US scholars and policymakers often refer to the idea of "religious freedom" or "religious liberty," Europeans use terminology drawn from international instruments, referring to the idea of "freedom of religion or belief." Far from being a mere terminological dispute, these differences indicate a very profound difficulty in arriving at a common notion of religious freedom. From this perspective, it is useful to note that the 2014 report of the US Commission on International Religious Freedom clarifies, we hope definitively, that for the commission, "religious freedom, freedom of religion and freedom of religion or belief interchangeably refer to the broad right to freedom of thought, conscience, and religion or belief protected under international human rights law."[31] Differences between the United States and European countries also appear with regard to the treatment of some religious groups. This difficulty is evidenced in the 2014 report of the U.S. Commission on International Religious Freedom, which dedicates a specific paragraph to the Western European countries, indicating violations of religious freedom within some of them.[32]

3. Conclusions

As Elizabeth Shakman Hurd has maintained, the promotion and protection of religious freedom is a more complex and difficult phenomenon than the mere approval of regulations and the creation of institutions dedicated to this purpose.[33] However, in this author's opinion, the sole case of institutions expressly dedicated to the protection and promotion of the right of religious freedom must not be seen solely in a negative light.[34] It is undeniable that, particularly within international organizations, it is increasingly difficult to promote

31 US Commission on International Religious Freedom, *Annual Report 2014*, p. 1. The expression "freedom of religion or belief" was used also in previous reports.

32 At the beginning of the paragraph the Commission mentions the cases that raise more concern: "These include restrictions on, and efforts to restrict, certain forms of religious expression (particularly dress and visible symbols, ritual slaughter and religious circumcision); governmental monitoring of disfavored groups pejoratively labeled 'cults' or 'sects', lack of accommodation of religious objections; and the potential use of hate speech laws against peaceful expression of belief." *Ibid.*, p. 163. Probably, influenced by these remarks, on May 9, 2014 Steve Stockman introduced a new bill in the House of Representatives, the "European Union Religious Freedom Act" with the specific goal to include within the text of the International Religious Freedom Act the explicit mentioning of four restrictions of religious freedom connected to: "1) homeschooling; 2) religious methods of meat production; 3) circumcision; 4) wearing religious garbs." See 113th Congress, 2nd session, H.R. 4650, *European Union Religious Freedom Act – To amend the International Religious Freedom Act of 1998 to include several additions to the many forms of violations of the right to religious freedom.*

33 Elizabeth Shakman Hurd, *Religious Freedom, American-style*, p. 241.

34 Elizabeth Shakman Hurd develops an argument against this stance. For her: "In positing the primacy of *religious* identity and difference over the social, political and economic ties and affiliations, international religious freedom advocacy accentuates and rigidifies religious divisions, making them more politically salient – and potentially more socially divisive. As a discursive framework and a language of political

shared policies on religious freedom. As Asma Jahangir, former Special rapporteur for religious freedom at the United Nations, recalled, if the regulation contained in Article 18 of the Universal Declaration of Human Rights was proposed today, it would probably not be approved.[35] This is because of the differences among the various states, and the initiatives of some actors – which, as we have seen, are often influenced by religious groups themselves – that aim to displace a center of gravity that is perceived as being overly-oriented toward the West and conceptions of liberal individualism. At the same time, even in Western societies, parallel and conflictual approaches face off against one another.

On the one hand are arguments supporting notions of religious freedom that increasingly value the collective and institutional aspects,[36] and on the other hand approaches that tend to marginalize the role of religion in the public sphere are making strides, partially due to the advancement of the secularization process. These two movements are opposed, yet parallel and simultaneous. With a healthy realism, we therefore need to remember the resources and institutions that could help contribute to the improvement, even minimal, of the protection and promotion of the right of religious freedom on a global scale. It is not an easy exercise, considering the increasingly evident crisis of multilateral institutions and international systems in their political and legal aspects.[37] The protection and promotion of the right to religious freedom is not exempted from this crisis, especially in its international dimension.[38]

We might ask ourselves if it is still possible to imagine the existence of institutions whose major task is the promotion and protection of religious freedom in today's international arena.[39] The more fragmented international regimes become and the more religions assume a role of transnational identity that challenges the ties of identification and loyalty that citizens have with the national states, the more difficult it is to answer this question.[40]

action, advocacy for religious freedom obfuscates complex political realities and obscures diverse and multiform religious affiliation and practices," *ibid.*, p. 241.

35 The statement is referred by Allen Hertzke: "Former United Nations Rapporteur on Freedom of Religion and Belief, Asma Jahangir, commented that the International covenant on religious freedom might not pass if proposed today." Allen Hertzke lists the political and social changes which are at the basis of this statement: "In a number of ways the normative consensus embodied in the *Universal Declaration* is weakening at the very time that it should be growing. This flows from a variety of converging forces, from secularization to theocratic movements, from identity politics to authoritarian pushback," Allen D. Hertzke, "Religious Freedom in the World Today: Paradox and Promise," pp. 126–127.

36 Silvio Ferrari has noticed how this phenomenon is of particular importance for what may concern the topic of proselytism: "For decades, the individual dimension of religious freedom was prevalent [...]. Today the collective dimension of this right has re-emerged forcefully, reaffirmed, for example, in recent UN resolutions on the defamation of religion. In the first view, each person receives his religion from the community into which he is born. Proselytism, if carried out in a correct manner, is always licit in the first case; it may not be in the second." Silvio Ferrari, *Proselytism and Human Rights*, in John Witte jr., Frank Alexander (ed.), *Christianity and Human Rights. An Introduction* (Cambridge: Cambridge University Press, 2010), p. 265.

37 Henry Kissinger, *World Order: Reflections on the Character of Nations and the Course of History* (New York: Penguin Press, 2014), (in which Kissinger argues that we are living through a non-reversible crisis of the international order we have known after the Second World war).

38 See Heiner Bielefeldt, "Misperception of Freedom of Religion or Belief," *Human Rights Quarterly* 35, no. 1, (2013): pp. 33–68.

39 Romeo Astorri, "E' ancora possibile una politica ecclesiastica? Tra 'caso italiano' e contesto europeo e internazionale," *Quaderni di Diritto e Politica Ecclesiastica*, 1, (2014): pp. 261–278.

40 On this issue see Silvio Ferrari, "Tra geo-diritti e teo-diritti. Riflessioni sulle religioni come centri transnazionali di identità," *Quaderni di Diritto e Politica Ecclesiastica*, 1, (2007): pp. 3–14 and also Mark

It is obviously impossible (perhaps not even desirable) to appeal to a right of religious freedom that one would necessarily want to be applied everywhere, according to the same characteristics and in the same ways. Those aiming for a uniform protection of the right of religious freedom on a global level risk bitter disappointment. Similarly, with regard to religious freedom, it is unthinkable that policies dedicated to its promotion can be separated from the short and medium-term political interests of the states and agencies or organs that promote them.[41] In the face of violence against many religious minorities in various parts of the world, it remains in any case desirable to coordinate, as broadly as possible, state and non-state actors who are committed to putting a stop to such violations of a fundamental right.[42] From this perspective, the approval of the International Religious Freedom Act should be considered a positive event if it succeeds in pushing an increasing number of countries to converge around this objective, and to influence supranational institutions. What remains certain is the epistemological problem of an appropriate definition of the notion of religious freedom[43] – a political one connected to its possible instrumentalization, or a legal one related to the forms and institutions most suitable for its protection and promotion. In any case, in the face of violence, particularly the most serious kind,[44] even a mere "humanitarian" action – which could be enacted by a possible cooperation between the United States, European countries, and any others who want to be part of it – would be welcomed as a success. It should not be forgotten that fighting religious persecution is not the same as promoting the right of religious freedom,[45] which instead requires a true agenda.[46]

Juergensmeyer, *Global Rebellion: Religious Challenges to the Secular State, from Christian Militias to al Qaeda* (Berkeley: University of California Press, 2008).

41 See on this issue the ambiguous relationship with China and its continuous violation of the right to religious freedom. Carol L. Hamrin, 'A New Framework For Promoting Religious Freedom in China', *The Brandywine Review of Faith & International Affairs* 3, no. 1, (2005): pp. 3–10.

42 See Knox Thames, "A Global Response to Religious Freedom Violations," *Georgetown Journal of International Affairs*, 23/1/2014, available at: http://goo.gl/skaiaQ.

43 Winnifred F. Sullivan, *The Impossibility of Religious Freedom* (Princeton: Princeton University Press, 2007). See also Saba Mahmood, "Religious Freedom, the Minority Question and Geopolitics in the Middle East," *Comparative Studies in Societies and History* 15, no. 2, (2012): pp. 418–446.

44 Enough would be to read the *Report on the Protection of Civilians in Armed Conflict in Iraq: 6 July–10 September 2014* of Office of the High Commissioner for human rights of the United Nations, available at: http://goog.gl/odCkyK. On the topic of restrictions to religious freedom and persecutions see also Brian J. Grim, and Roger Finke, *The Price of Freedom Denied: Religious Persecution and Conflict in the 21st Century* (New York: Cambridge University Press, 2011).

45 This is a distinction made by Thomas Farr for the US context. As Farr writes: "Opposing persecution and freeing foreigners, however successfully, is not the same as advancing religious freedom," Thomas F. Farr, *World of Faith and Freedom. Why International Religious Liberty is Vital to American National Security*, p. 17.

46 See Malcom Evans, 'Advancing Freedom of Religion or Belief: Agendas for Change', *Oxford Journal of Law and Religion* 1, no. 1, (2012): pp. 5–14.

References

Astorri Romeo, "E' ancora possibile una politica ecclesiastica? Tra "caso italiano" e contesto europeo e internazionale," *Quaderni di Diritto e Politica Ecclesiastica*, 1, (2014): pp. 261–278.

Barry, Ellen, "U.S. Court Issues Summons to Modi Lawsuit Over 2002 Riots," *The New York Times*, 26/9/2014.

Baird, John, "Address to the United Nations General Assembly," 26/9/2011, available at: www.international.gc.ca.

Baird, Johnn, "Address at Office of Religious Freedom Stakeholder Consultation," 3/10/2011, available at: www.international.gc.ca.

Bielefeldt, Heiner, "Misperception of Freedom of Religion or Belief," *Human Rights Quarterly* 35, no. 1, (2013): pp. 33–68.

Chase, Steven, "New Religious-freedom Watchdog Faces Uphill Battle," *The Globe and Mail*, 7/6/2013.

Evans, Malcolm, "Advancing Freedom of Religion or Belief: Agendas for Change," *Oxford Journal of Law and Religion* 1, no. 1, (2012): pp. 5–14.

Farr, Thomas F., *Testimony before the House Committee on Oversight and Government Reform-Subcommittee on National Security* within the context of the hearing *Examining the Government's Record on Implementing the International Religious Freedom Act*, 13/6/2013.

Farr, Thomas F., "Obama Administration Sidelines Religious Freedom Policy," *The Washington Post*, 25/6/2010.

Farr, Thomas F., *World of Faith and Freedom. Why International Religious Liberty is Vital to American National Security* (New York: Oxford University Press, 2008).

Ferrari, Silvio, *Proselytism and Human Rights*, in John Witte jr., and Frank Alexander (ed.), *Christianity and Human Rights. An Introduction* (Cambridge: Cambridge University Press, 2010), pp. 253–266.

Ferrari, Silvio, "Tra geo-diritti e teo-diritti. Riflessioni sulle religioni come centri transnazionali di identità," *Quaderni di Diritto e Politica Ecclesiastica*, 1, (2007): pp. 3–14.

Grim, Brian J., and Finke, Roger, *The Price of Freedom Denied: Religious Persecution and Conflict in the 21st Century* (New York: Cambridge University Press, 2011).

Hamrin, Carol L., "A New Framework For Promoting Religious Freedom in China," *The Brandywine Review of Faith & International Affairs* 3, no. 1, (2005): pp. 3–10.

Hertzke, Allen D., "Religious Freedom in the World Today: Paradox and Promise," in Glendon Mary A., and Zacher Hans F (eds.), *Universal Rights in a World of Diversity. The case of Religious Freedom* (Vatican City: Pontifical Academy of Social Sciences, 2012), pp. 108–133.

Joustra, Robert, "Three Rival Versions of Religious Freedom: What Canada's Office of Religious Freedom Can Teach Us About Principled Pluralism," *The Review of Faith and International Affairs* 12, no. 3 (2014): pp. 41–54.

Juergensmeyer, Mark, *Global Rebellion: Religious Challenges to the Secular State, from Christian Militias to al Qaeda* (Berkeley: University of California Press, 2008).

Kindopp, Jason, "Principled Engagement in China," *The Brandywine Review of Faith and International Affairs* 1, no. 1 (2003): pp. 21–30.

Kissinger, Henry, *World Order: Reflections on the Character of Nations and the Course of History* (New York: Penguin Press, 2014).

Leo, Leonard, and Argue, Don, "International Religious Freedom: Why It matters and How to Protect It," *International Affairs Review* 20, no. 1 (2011): pp. 1–12.

Lantos Sweet, Katrina, *Testimony Before the National Security Subcommittee of the House Committee on Oversight and Government Reform* within the context of the hearing *Examining the Government's Record on Implementing the International Religious Freedom Act*, 13/6/2013.

Mahmood, Saba, "Religious Freedom, the Minority Question and Geopolitics in the Middle East," *Comparative Studies in Societies and History* 15, no. 2, (2012): pp. 418–446.

Mann, James, "Why Narendra Modi was Banned from the U.S.," *The Wall Street Journal*, 2/5/2014.

Office of the High Commissioner for human rights of the United Nations, *Report on the Protection of Civilians in Armed Conflict in Iraq: 6 July–10 September 2014*, available at: http://goog.gl/odCkyK.

Payton, Laura, "Canada Giving $ 1.2M for Religious Freedom in Nigeria, Central Asia," *CBS News*, 26/8/2013, available at: http://en.africatime.com/external?url=http://www.cbc.ca/news/politics/story/2013/08/26/pol-office-of-religious-freedom-projects.html.

Shakman Hurd, Elizabeth, "Religious Freedom, American-style," *Quaderni di Diritto e Politica Ecclesiastica* 1, (2014): pp. 231–242.

Shakman Hurd, Elizabeth, "The Hegemony of Religious Freedom," *The Globe and Mail*, 17/10/2012.

Shakman Hurd, Elizabeth, "Believing in Religious Freedom," *The Immanent Frame*, 1/3/2012, available at: http://blogs.ssrc.org/tif/2012/03/01/believing-in-religious-freedom.

Sharma, Arvind, "Religious Freedom, Compliments of the West," *The Mark News*, 6/12/2011.

Simpson, Jeffrey, "The Office of Religious Freedom, More Conservative Slice and Dice," *The Globe and Mail*, 23/2/2013.

Sinha, Shreeya, "Indian Leader Narendra Modi, Once Unwelcomed in U.S., Get Rock Star Reception," *The New York Times*, 27/9/2014.

Sullivan, Winnifred F., *The Impossibility of Religious Freedom* (Princeton: Princeton University Press, 2007).

Thames, Knox, "A Global Response to Religious Freedom Violations," *Georgetown Journal of International Affairs*, 23/1/2014, available at: http://goo.gl/skaiaQ.

U.S. Government Accountability Office, *Report to Congressional Committees-International Religious Freedom Act. State Department and Commission are Implementing Responsibilities but Need to Improve Interaction*, GAO-13-196, March 2013, pp. 1–66, available at: www.gao.gov/products/GAO-13-196.

U.S. Commission on International Religious Freedom, *Annual Report 2014*.

Wallace, James C., and Wiseman, Richelle, "The Promise of Canada's Office of Religious Freedom," *The Review of Faith and International Affairs* 11, no. 3 (2013): pp. 52–60.

Weigel, George, "Why U.S. International Religious Freedom Policy Fails," *Catholic Exchange*, 6/8/2013.

Postscript

Since the publication of the Italian edition of this book, the debate on the international promotion and protection of religious freedom has seen a significant increase in interest, and the debate has been enriched by many voices. Some are new, and some are highlighting and clarifying points already raised by various authors. As I have tried to show, over the years the American model, represented by the International Religious Freedom Act, has to various degrees influenced legislation in other countries. The Obama administration has also contributed to its improvement by approving the "Frank R. Wolf International Religious Freedom Act," which amended the original International Religious Freedom Act of 1998. It is worth mentioning that the Act inserts "specific targeting of non-theists, humanists, and atheists because of their beliefs," clarifying that American action in the field must also be addressed to these groups. The Act also established the new category of "entities of particular concern," to address the problem of non-state actors and groups that threaten international religious freedom. It also changed the structure of the International Religious Freedom Office at the State Department to guarantee a stable number of employees working on religious freedom, and established the requirement that all Foreign Service Officers receive training on international religious freedom. Finally, it is worth mentioning that the Act also gives more relevance to the Ambassador at Large for International Religious Freedom, who now reports directly to the Secretary of State. All of these are significant modernizations made to the original text of the International Religious Freedom Act, intended to improve its application. Meanwhile in Europe, in May 2016 the President of the European Commission appointed the first "Special Envoy for the Promotion and Protection of Freedom of Religion or Belief outside the European Union." The appointment of former European Commission member Dr. Ján Figel came at a crucial time, when the EU was called to review the Guidelines approved in 2013. These are all important technical improvements. On the other hand, it must be admitted that the politicization that had very much influenced the Canadian and Italian experiences with the promotion and protection of religious freedom led to their collapse. These experiences are an important reminder that the goal of promoting and protecting religious freedom must be shared by the major players in the political spectrum or – to put it quite simply – it won't work, but instead sideline the efforts of those who really believe in religious freedom. While it is possible to see how the American model has inspired other countries over the years, today it is my impression that this route will not be an easy one. Not because we are moving "beyond" religious freedom,[1] but because America probably does not believe anymore (or enough) in religious freedom.[2] It has not been enough to warn scholars and policymakers of the dangers of concentrating authority in only one set of institutions. I think that if there is anything to be learned from our current experiences in the world, it is the dangers of authoritarian states exploiting religion for other purposes. Here, the words of Brett Scharffs are to be heeded very carefully:

> If we fear statism, monistic states that recognize no limits on their authority, and view rights as gifts bestowed by the states (gifts that may also be taken back by the state), then we need something like a dualist outlook, which differentiates between the sphere of state authority and other spheres of non-state authority. The intellectual resources for a dualist understanding of limited state power is rooted, historically and intellectually, in religious ways of viewing the world. Without religion, I'm not sure we have the intellectual, moral or philosophical resources to resist the imperial logic of statism.[3]

Religion and religious freedom are not a panacea for every possible problem that societies face, but can be useful in defending the intermediate institutions of civil society and the conscience of the individual. Today, advocacy on behalf of religious freedom is becoming more difficult for the Western states as well. This is candidly admitted in the 2017 interim report of the European Parliament Intergroup on Freedom of Religion or Belief and Religious Tolerance:

> We witness a trade-off between economic, in particular trade-related, interests and human rights policies. Similarly, we notice hesitance to raise difficult human rights issues with countries of strategic interest, be it because of their dominant position in other parts of the world, or their role in helping the EU cope with migration pressures.[4]

This is an important statement, a recognition of a real pragmatic inability to promote and protect religious freedom in many parts of the world due to the concrete situations that public institutions often face. Of course it is not always so. Some states simply prefer to ignore violations and pursue other interests instead of promoting human rights and religious freedom. Therefore, on this issue I join those who argue that in fact there is no such large international machinery in place to promote and protect religious freedom:

1 See Elizabeth Shakman Hurd, *Beyond Religious Freedom. The New Global Politics of Religion* (Princeton: Princeton University Press, 2015). See also the critiques advanced to this approach in Daniel Philpott and Timothy S. Shah, "In defence of religious freedom: new critics of a beleaguered human right," *Journal of Law and Religion* 32, no. 3, (2016): pp. 380–395.

2 This claim has been also made for what concerns the protection of religious freedom within the United States. See Steven D. Smith, *The Rise and Decline of American Religious Freedom* (Cambridge: Harvard University Press, 2014).

3 Brett Scharffs, "Why Religious Freedom? Why the Religiously Committed, the Religiously Indifferent and those Hostile to Religion Should Care, forthcoming *Brigham Young University Law Review*, available at: https://papers.ssrn.com/sol3/papers.cfm?abstract_id=2911086, p. 22.

4 European Parliament Intergroup on Freedom of Religion or Belief and Religious Tolerance, *Interim Report 2017*, p. 11.

> In a world in which large numbers of people suffer from arbitrary and often grotesque restrictions and violence at least partially because of their religious identity and practice, religious freedom and religious freedom policies are of little interest to the powerful, including, increasingly, the government of the United States.[5]

To this extent, the presidential election of November 2016 has likely opened up a new world for international religious freedom and for relations between the United States and Europe. Disengagement from world affairs and alliance with regimes that are serious violators of fundamental rights is not a promising foundation.[6] Theoretical and practical questions still remain, and the promotion and protection of religious freedom should not be exempt from any critique addressed to similar enterprises in other fields of human rights:

> Like all policies, religious freedom admits of controversies. Should it be pursued unilaterally or multilaterally? Should it be isolated as a human rights policy or incorporated into the high politics of alliance, diplomacy, and counterterrorism? Have religious freedom policies succeeded in improving religious freedom around the world?[7]

These are all fundamental questions which have been not settled and should continue to be asked. But are the doubts and the open questions that remain in the debate on international religious freedom enough to do away with notion of religious freedom itself, leaving it behind and moving on? It seems that we could all at least agree on the need to promote and protect the cases with worst violations, tackling regimes that jail people for what they believe and what they preach. This should be a basic commitment for courageous and serious people. Will we be able to meet the challenge?

[5] Daniel Philpott and Timothy S. Shah, "In defense of religious freedom: new critics of a beleaguered human right," *Journal of Law and Religion* 31, no. 3 (2016), p. 388.

[6] Michael Posner, "Trump abandons the human-rights agenda," *The New Yorker*, 26/5/2017, available at: www.newyorker.com/news/news-desk/trump-abandons-the-human-rights-agenda?intcid=mod-latest.

[7] Daniel Philpott, Timothy S. Shah, "In defense of religious freedom: new critics of a beleaguered human right," p. 394.

Index

For Product Safety Concerns and Information please contact our EU representative GPSR@taylorandfrancis.com Taylor & Francis Verlag GmbH, Kaufingerstraße 24, 80331 München, Germany